re:CONNECT

SPIRITUAL EXERCISES
TO DEVELOP
INTIMACY WITH GOD

DAVID SHERBINO

Re:connect: Spiritual Exercises to Develop Intimacy with God

Published by:
Castle Quay Books
Pickering, Ontario
Tel: (416) 573-3249
E-mail: info@castlequaybooks.com
www.castlequaybooks.com

Cover design by Burst Impressions
Printed at Essence Publishing, Belleville, Ontario

Library and Archives Canada Cataloguing in Publication

Sherbino, David
     Re:connect : spiritual exercises to develop intimacy with
God / David Sherbino.

Includes bibliographical references.
Issued also in electronic format.
ISBN 978-1-927355-20-6

     1. Spiritual life—Christianity. 2. Spiritual exercises.
I. Title. II. Title: Reconnect. III. Title: Spiritual exercises to
develop intimacy with God.

BV4501.3.S54 2013   248.4   C2013-900316-9

CASTLE QUAY BOOKS

Well done!
Most books talk about the importance of prayer.
Your book tells people how to pray.
Sorely needed.

Don Morrison, Former COO,
BlackBerry at Research in Motion (RIM)

CONTENTS

CONTENTS

INTRODUCTION

In recent years the spiritual disciplines have become a topic of great interest and discussion. Some will attest that the disciplines help them to enter into a more intimate relationship with God. There are others who want to, but do not know how, to integrate them into their daily life. It seems that the issue of time is the greatest road block in the development of the disciplines as an integral aspect of life. We are so busy 'doing' we do not have enough time to 'be still' in the presence of God to discover intimacy with him. We need to find a way to 'reconnect' with God.

This workbook is designed to help us to do that. The focus is on the discipline of prayer which is simply listening to God and then responding to God. One request of the disciples of Jesus was that he teach them to pray. They heard him teach, they saw him perform miracles and they witnessed his life of prayer. Ultimately they came to the conclusion that if they were to continue the ministry he began it could only be accomplished through an intimate relationship with God. They knew they needed to stay connected to God.

If you desire to draw closer or reconnect with God these exercise will help you. The material is designed in such a way that the daily exercises will help you not only learn about the discipline but actually experience doing the discipline. This workbook covers a period of seven weeks and if you follow it carefully you will notice a change in your spiritual practice and devotion.

We begin the exercises with the discipline of 'Silence and Solitude'. This practice enables us to learn to be still and to wait in quiet expectation so we can hear God as he speaks to us. The second discipline is learning to listen to God speak before we speak to him. This comes through the ancient practice of 'Holy Listening'. The third prayer discipline is learning to 'Pray the Scriptures'. These are scriptural texts that have formed the prayers of God's people for generations. The Fourth discipline is learning to pray 'Prayers of Confession' using an ancient form of prayer called 'The Prayer of Examen'. The fifth discipline is focused on 'Lament'. Most of us go through times or pain and anguish, the 'Prayers of Lament' enable us to be authentic before God as we cry out to him. In the sixth discipline we encounter 'Petitionary Prayers'. This is where we intercede for ourselves and for others. The final discipline is 'Thanksgiving and Praise', with a focus on the names of God as the basis of our prayer.

A final chapter is devoted to an explanation of the church year with exercises to help direct your prayers during these seasons of the year.

The key to experiencing the book is to complete the exercises each day.

Enjoy!

SILENCE & SOLITUDE

'Be still and know that I am God...'

Ps.46:10

As we explore various spiritual disciplines that will help to draw us closer to God we begin with silence and solitude. Devoted followers of the Lord have practiced silence and solitude throughout the ages as a means of deliberately making space in their busy schedules to listen and hear the voice of God. Without silence and solitude we will never be able to fully enter into intimacy with God simply because so many other voices are contending for our attention and commitment.

Basil Pennington used the metaphor of a pond to describe the importance of stillness in order to pay attention to God. When you throw a stone into a pond, he said, the stone will create ripples that reach to the shore, all way around — but only if the pond is still. When the pond is quiet and still, the impact of the stone can be seen over the entire surface. But when the pond is not still, when the surface of the water is already ruffled and tossed, the splash of the stone will go undetected. Where the wind has disturbed the surface, the stone can't be disturbing. Where a storm is present, there is so much commotion already going on that no one will notice a few waves more or less as they will be lost in the frantic motion of the surface. Stillness is always the prerequisite for receptivity.

In our world it seems we are constantly surrounded by noise and by people. In fact we regularly speak of 'noise pollution'. It seems to be very difficult, if not impossible, to be still and experience the presence of God. In addition to this we are driven by the compulsion to be busy as many see their value and worth attached to what they do. So to be quiet and to be alone for periods of time seems to be less than productive and for some completely meaningless, since we are perceived to be doing nothing. However if we want to hear God's voice we must move into surrendered intimacy with him. Then we are able to listen and hear the still soft voice of God.

Be Still

Be still for the presence of Lord the Holy One is here.
Come bow before Him now with reverence and fear.
In Him no sin is found, we stand on holy ground.
Be still, for the presence of the Lord, the Holy One is here.

Be still, for the glory of the Lord is shining all around.
He burns with holy fire, with splendour He is crowned.
How awesome is the sight, our radiant King of Light!
Be still, for the glory of the Lord is shining all around.

Be still, for the power of the Lord is moving in this place.
He comes to cleanse and heal, to minister His grace
No work and too hard for Him, in faith receive from Him,
Be still, for the power of the Lord is moving in this place. [1]

THE EXAMPLE OF JESUS
The following scriptures reveal that Jesus practiced silence and solitude as a regular aspect of his life.

Matthew 4:1. We are told that the Holy Spirit led Jesus into a period of fasting and solitude while in the desert. After this particular experience Jesus returned to Galilee "in the power of the Spirit" (Luke 4:14)

Matthew 14:23. After Jesus ministered to the multitudes he sent them away and he went up to a mountain by himself to pray. Jesus was completely alone. He sent both the crowd and his disciples away so that he could be alone with God.

Mark 1:35. Jesus had been teaching in the synagogue and healing people of various diseases. This ministry continued into the night. The next morning while it was still dark he went off to a lonely place to spend time alone in the presence of the Father. If Jesus waited till later in the morning he would never have the time nor the opportunity to be alone in silence and solitude as the demands of people were constant.

It should be obvious as we reflect on these texts that if we want to live more like Jesus, we will need to practice silence and solitude even as he did.

THE PLACE OF SILENCE

The Bible praises the virtue of silence. Proverbs tell us that "where words are many transgression is not lacking, but the one who restrains his lips is prudent" (Proverbs 10:19. And "even a fool, if he keeps silent, is considered wise" (Proverbs 17:28). In the New Testament, James goes as far as to say "if anyone does not fall short in speech, that person is a perfect individual" (James 3:2).

Jesus also gave a strong warning about our speech. He declared that "on the Day of Judgment people will have to give an account for every idle word they have spoken. For by your words you will be saved, and by your words you will be condemned" (Matthew 12:36).

C.S. Lewis in the Screwtape Letters puts words in the mouth of the Devil to show that noise is the friend of the Devil. He states: "Music and silence-how I detest them both! How thankful we should be that ever since our father (that is Lucifer) entered hell, no square inch of infernal space and no amount of infernal time has been surrendered to either of those abominable forces, but has been occupied by, Noise-Noise, the grand dynamism, the audible expression of all that is exalted, ruthless and virile – Noise which alone defends us from silly qualms, despairing scruples and impossible desires. We will make the whole universe a noise in the end. We have already made great strides in this direction as regards the earth. The melodies and silences of Heaven will be shut down in the end". [2]

The practice of silence does not mean that we have to be constantly quiet and never say anything. At times silence is destructive and painful, for example when we give someone 'the silent treatment'. To practice the discipline of silence, we must know when to speak, to whom to speak, and the right way to speak

The apostle Paul stated we must speak only about "whatever is honourable, whatever is just, whatever is pure, whatever is gracious, and anything worthy of praise" (Philippians 4:8). The Psalmist states: "whoever of you loves life and desires to see many good days, keep your tongue from evil and your lips from speaking lies" (Psalm 34:12-13).

3

Since the primary purpose of silence is to help us grow in the love and knowledge of Christ, we must be selective in our conversations and sometimes sacrifice our desire to speak especially if our words are hurtful or destructive.

It is also important to practice silence when we are speaking to others. We do this when we listen to someone. James writes "Let everyone be quick to hear and slow to speak" (James 1:19).

THE PLACE OF SOLITUDE

The Gospel records tell us Jesus took significant periods of time away from ministry and -people simply to be alone with God. At the beginning of his ministry Jesus went into the wilderness for a period of 40 days to pray and fast. (Matthew 4:1-11)

Later Jesus taught his followers to do the very same thing. After ministering to the crowds he had the disciples get into a boat and cross over to the other side of the lake where they would be alone away from the crowd and their persistent demands. (Matthew 14:13-33) Jesus knew the disciples needed time alone to allow God to renew them so they could continue their ministry empowered and energized by the Holy Spirit. They needed to "come apart" before they "came apart".

Jesus also encouraged his followers to be in a place of solitude when they prayed. He said when they were praying they were to go into a closet to pray to their Father in secret. (Matthew 6:1-8)

Henri Nouwen states: "Solitude is difficult for many people, because they don't know what to do in the solitude. Most of us are used to being very busy and productive but in solitude we seem to do nothing. For those who have used productivity as the basis for their self-worth this becomes a drastic if not radical departure from their way of living. But in solitude we are not completely alone, Christ is with us, and we are deepening our relationship with him.

We enter into solitude first of all to meet our Lord and to be with him and him alone. Our primary task in solitude, therefore, is not to pay undue attention to the many faces which assail us, but to keep, the eyes of our mind and heart on him who is our Divine Saviour. Only in the context of grace can we face our sin; only in the place of healing do we dare to show our wounds; only with a single minded attention to Christ can we give up our clinging fears and face our own true nature. As we come to realize that it is not we who live, but Christ who lives in us, that he is our true self, we can slowly let our compulsions melt away and begin to experience the freedom of the children of God.

Solitude is thus a place of purification and transformation, the place of the great struggle and the great encounter. Solitude is not simply a means to an end. Solitude is its own end. It is the place for Christ remodels us in his own image and frees us from the victimizing compulsions of the world. Solitude is the place of our salvation. Hence, it is the place where we want to lead all who are seeking the light in this dark world. St. Anthony spent 20 years in isolation. When he left it he took his solitude with him and shared it with all who came to him. Those who saw him described him as balanced, gentle, and caring. He had become so Christ-like, so radiant with God's love, that his entire being was ministry". [3]

The exercises will provide an opportunity to practice some basic elements of silence and solitude and to discover some of the benefits of the discipline. Initially it may feel somewhat strange and unnatural, but if you stay with it you will come to appreciate and possibility even seek out regular times of silence and solitude. As a word of warning to those who are somewhat extroverted … 'this will be difficult'. To those who are somewhat introverted … 'this is a dream come true'.

PRACTICING SILENCE AND SOLITUDE

DAY 1: TO HEAR AND LISTEN TO THE VOICE OF GOD

There are many voices seeking our attention. In silence and solitude we distance ourselves from some of these voices so we can hear the voice of God.

Elijah stood on Mount Horeb where he heard God speak in a gentle whisper.

"The Lord said, "Go out and stand on the mountain in the presence of the Lord, for the Lord is about to pass by".

Then a great and powerful wind tore the mountains apart and shattered the rocks before the Lord, but the Lord was not in the wind. After the wind there was an earthquake, but the Lord was not in the earthquake. After the earthquake came a fire, but the Lord was not in the fire. And after the fire came a gentle whisper. When Elijah heard it, he pulled his cloak over his face and went out and stood at the mouth of the cave. 1Kings 19:11-13

Habakkuk, struggling with God's sovereign plan in dealing with a ruthless nation, stood at the guard post keeping watch to see what God would say to him.

DAY 1

"I will stand at my watch and station myself on the ramparts; I will look to see what he will say to me, and what answer I am to give to this complaint". Habakkuk 2:1.

Of course it is not absolutely necessary to be in silence and solitude to hear the voice of God, otherwise we would never perceive his promptings in daily life. But there seems to be times when we need to be alone without any distractions so that we can hear God speak to us.

EXERCISE:

1. Find a place that is quiet and free from distractions. Make this your regular place of 'sanctuary'.

2. Sit quietly before the Lord and offer this time to God expressing your desire to be with him. Say nothing but just sit in silence for five minutes.

3. Read 1 Kings 19:1-18.

4. Record any thoughts that you have from this passage

5. Listen to hear the 'still small voice of God'.

6. Write out a prayer that expresses your desires as you identify with Elijah.

7. Conclude your time by sitting in silence for five minutes and then give thanks to God for his presence in your life.

DAY 2

DAY 2. TO BE RENEWED PHYSICALLY AND SPIRITUALLY

All of us need to be renewed inwardly and outwardly on a regular basis. In the creation story God rested on the seventh day and gave the command that we are to do the same. In other words God did not intend that we keep going day after day but that we need periods of rest and renewal on a regular basis.

Jesus understood this concept and taught it to his closest followers. In one account in the Gospels, Jesus and his disciples were ministering to the crowd and were so busy they did not even have time to eat lunch. Finally he said to the disciples they needed to have a break. "Come away by yourselves to a lonely place and rest a while" (Mark 6:31)

Many are caught up in a lifestyle of busyness. We have no time to rest. Even our weekends are filled with feverish activity and we wonder why we are so stressed out. We need to have regular periods of silence and solitude to renew our body and soul.

Henri Nouwen who was a busy academic had a six-month sabbatical at Genesee Abbey in New York. During that time he wrote about his experiences and the apparent paradoxes in the search for silence and solitude.

"While complaining about too many demands, I felt uneasy when none were made. While speaking about the burden of letter writing, an empty mailbox made me sad. While fretting about tiring lecture tours, I felt disappointed when there were no invitations. While speaking nostalgically about an empty desk, I feared the day when that would come true. In short: while desiring to be alone, I was frightened of being alone. The more I became aware of these paradoxes, the more I had indeed fallen in love with my own compulsions and illusions, and how much I needed to step back and wonder, "Is there a quiet stream underneath my fluctuating affirmations and rejections of my little world? Is there a still point where my life is anchored and from which I can reach out with hope and courage and confidence?' [4]

EXERCISE:

1. Take some time this week to look at your schedule. Do you regularly take time for rest and renewal? When did you do it last? What did you do? When you take time to rest and be renewed do you feel guilty?

2. Read Mark.6:30-56. What do you discover about Jesus as he ministers to people? How would you describe His approach to ministry?

3. Make a plan this week to take some time off. What will you do? When will you do it? When you have completed this exercise take a few moments to reflect upon your experience.

4. Will you make this a regular experience?

DAY 3

DAY 3. TO LEARN TO TRUST GOD

Most people like things to happen quickly and according to their timetable. And most often we are in a hurry. Dr. Archibald Hart a Christian psychologist suggests that our culture suffers from 'the hurry up sickness'.

John Ortburg states: "we will buy anything that promises to help us hurry. The best selling shampoo in America rose to the top because it combines shampoo and conditioned in one step, eliminating the need for all the time consuming rinsing people used to have to do…"

He goes on to say, "we worship at the shrine of the Golden Arches, not because they sell 'good food' or even 'cheap food'. But because it is 'fast food'. Even after fast food was introduced, people still had to park their cars, go inside, order, and take their food to a table, all of which took time. So we invented the Drive – Thro Lane to enable families to eat in their vans as nature intended." [5]

When things don't work out the way we hoped or expected we want to get busy and try to fix it. Sometimes we become anxious and upset. As long as we are busy doing something there is the feeling that it will work out because we are working it out. Perhaps we are just going around in circles.

Coming before God and waiting upon him in silence and solitude is really an act of trust that God in his sovereign way will act in his time. David the Psalmist states "My soul waits in silence for God only; from Him is my salvation. He is my rock and my salvation, my stronghold; I shall not be greatly shaken….My soul waits in silence for God only, for my hope is from Him. He is my only rock and my salvation, my stronghold; I shall not be shaken…. Trust in him at all times O people; pour out your hearts to him, for God is our refuge" (Ps.62:1-2; 5-6.; 8).

EXERCISE:

1. Slowly read Psalm. 62

2. Having read the text sit in silence before God.

3. Write in your journal any thoughts that come from the reading.

4. What does it mean for you to trust in God as you contemplate your situation in life today?

Is it difficult for you to leave this with God?

What do you think He wants you to do?

5. Read Philippians. 4:6-7. Write a prayer that applies this truth to your life.

6. Memorize Philippians4:6-7 and recall it during the day especially when you become anxious.

DAY 4. TO DEVELOP SENSITIVITY TOWARD OTHERS

When we are constantly with others it can become extremely demanding and draining upon us. Regularly we hear of people suffering from 'burn out'. This is a place where we are drained and we feel we have nothing more to give. We are emotionally 'flat lined'. In silence and solitude we can be renewed physically, emotionally and spiritually so that we can go back into the mainstream of life and minister 'in the name of Jesus'. Most will not be called to live a life of separation from society; we are called to live in community, but this is a demanding place simply because people are demanding.

As we spend time alone with God, He will renew us and enable us to minister to others with the same tenderness and compassion He showed. Without this time of renewal we have a tendency to become 'weary in well doing', and begin to resent the demands people make on us. When Jesus saw the needs of the people He always showed compassion toward them, for He saw them as 'sheep without a shepherd'.

Thomas Merton stated, "solitude is not turning one's back on the world; it is turning one's face toward God".[6] When we do this we have a different attitude toward people. We start to listen to them, to be less judgmental of them, and to be fully present with them.

DAY
4

9

EXERCISE:

1. Take five minutes as you enter into silence to repeat the 'Jesus Prayer' "Lord Jesus Christ, Son of God, have mercy on me a sinner'.

2. Having prayed this prayer take another five minutes to allow the meaning of the prayer to resonate with your soul. What does the mercy of God mean to you?

3. Read the parable of the Pharisee and the Tax Collector. Lk.18:9-14

4. Which one do you identify with most closely? How will this story help you to develop sensitivity toward people? What next steps do you need to take?

5. Think about some of the people you will encounter today. What resources of grace do you need to be 'Christ' to them? As you pray ask the Lord to enable you in very specific ways to be sensitive toward them.

DAY 5. FACING TEMPTATION

DAY 5

Before Jesus began his ministry he was led by the Spirit into the desert and for forty days in silence and solitude he struggled with the Devil. Matthew records the three different temptations Jesus encountered which were intended to entice Him away from His calling. In his book 'In the Name of Jesus' Henri Nouwen discusses these three temptations as ones we all face in our Christian journey.

The first temptation Nouwen declares is the temptation to be relevant: "If you are the Son of God, turn these stones into bread.' (Matthew 4:3) In ministry we face this similar temptation. He states "Are we not called to do something that makes a difference in people's lives? Aren't we called to heal the sick, feed the hungry and alleviate the suffering of the poor? Jesus was faced with the same questions, but when he was asked to prove his power as the Son of God by the relevant power of changing stones into bread, he clung to his mission to proclaim the word and said, "Human beings live not by bread alone but by every word that comes from the mouth of God." [7]

Perhaps in our attempt to be relevant when many in ministry feel that what they are doing makes absolutely no difference in the lives of people we want to appear relevant by meeting the needs of people. Nouwen challenges us to be careful and to be aware of this temptation which on the surface seems to be so subtle. For Nouwen the "leader of the future will be one who dares to claim his irrelevance in the contemporary world as a divine vocation that allows him or her to enter into a deep solidarity with the anguish underlying all the glitter of success and to bring the light of Jesus there." [8]

The second temptation is to be spectacular, to do something that would win him the approval and applause of the crowd. "If you are the Son of God, throw yourself down from the highest pinnacle...He will command his angels concerning you and they will lift you up in their hands so that you will not strike your foot against a stone." (Matthew 4:6) Nouwen states "Jesus refused to be a stunt man. He did not come to prove himself … When you look at today's Church, it is easy to see the prevalence of individualism among ministers and priests. Not too many of us have a vast repertoire of skills to be proud of, but most of us still feel that if we have anything at all to show, it is something we have to do solo….Stardom and individual heroism, which are such obvious aspects of our competitive society, are not at all alien to the Church. There too the dominant image is that of the self - made man or woman who can do it all alone." [9]

The third temptation is the temptation of power. "Again the devil took him to a very high mountain and showed him all the kingdoms of the world and their splendour. All this I will give you if you will bow down and worship me" (Matthew 4:8-9) Nouwen writes "One of the greatest ironies of the history of Christianity is that its leaders constantly gave in to the temptation of power…The temptation to consider power an apt instrument for the proclamation of the Gospel is the greatest of all. We keep hearing from others, as well as saying to ourselves, that having power-provided it is used in the service of God and your fellow human beings-is a good thing. With this rationalization, crusades took place; inquisitions were organized; Indians were enslaved; positions of great influence were desired; Episcopal palaces were built; and much moral manipulation of conscience was engaged in.

What makes the temptation to power so seemingly irresistible? Maybe it is that power offers an easy substitute for the hard task of love. It seems easier to be God than to love God, easier to control people than to love people, easier to own life than to love life.

One thing is clear; the temptation of power is greatest when intimacy is a threat. Much Christian leadership is exercised by people who do not know how to develop healthy, intimate relationships and have opted for power and control instead. Many Christian empire-builders have been people unable to give and receive love." [10]

We are told that at the conclusion of the three temptations 'the devil left him and angels came and ministered to him". (Matthew 4:11)

Jesus did not succumb to the temptations, but that does not mean they were over. At the end of his ministry we see the challenge Jesus would face. Alone in the garden of Gethsemane with his three closest followers asleep Jesus again faced an incredible challenge. Would he accept the will of the Father and walk in obedience to the cross or evade the ones who sought his death. The agony was so great that 'his sweat was like drops of blood falling to the ground'. (Luke 22:46)

There will be times when we are alone and the silence is pervasive, that temptations will arise within us.

Solitude also brings periods of testing. We do not need to run from it, in fact there is a sense in which we can almost welcome it if we bring God with us into the situation. If we know the presence and power of the living Christ in our life then we know that he is with us and that 'He who is in us is greater than he who is in the world'. Not only will we grow through this experience but we will be victorious if we hold onto Christ.

EXERCISE:

1. Take some time to recall an experience where you faced temptation or testing that came in solitude. What was the experience like? What were the feelings you experienced?

2. Read the account of Jesus temptation Matthew 4:1-11 and his testing Luke 22:39-46.

3. As you recall your experience did you deal with it well? Do these two accounts of Jesus experience help you to see how you might deal with temptation and testing differently?

4. If you are dealing with some temptation or testing at this moment write out a prayer that expresses not only your struggle but also your desire.

5. Memorize 1 John 4:4. Make this your prayer and offer it several times during this day.

DAY 6. TO DEVELOP YOUR PRAYER LIFE

DAY
6

"Very early in the morning, while it was still dark, Jesus got up, left the house and went off to a solitary place, where he prayed." Mk.1:35

Henri Nouwen states: "in the middle of sentences loaded with action – healing suffering people, casting out devils, responding to inpatient disciples, traveling from town to town and preaching from synagogue to synagogue – we find these quiet words.

In the center of breathless activities we hear a restful breathing. Surrounded by hours of moving we find a moment of quiet stillness. In the heart of much involvement there are words of withdrawal. In the midst of action there is contemplation. And after much togeth-erness there is solitude. The more I read this nearly silent sentence locked in between the loud words of action, the more I have the sense that the secret of Jesus ministry is hidden in that lonely place where he went to pray, early in the morning, long before dawn

In a lonely place Jesus finds the courage to follow God's will and not his own; to speak God's words and not his own; to do God's work and not his own. He reminds us constantly: "I can do nothing by myself … my aim is to do and not my own well," but the will of him who sent me" (John 14:10). It is in the lonely place, where Jesus enters into intimacy with the father come that his ministry is born." [11]

In solitude Jesus was able to listen to the voice of the Father and not be directed by the needs and demands of the people. In prayer the first thing we need is to be silent before God so that we can hear Him speak to us.

Jesus also told his followers that when they prayed they were to 'go into their room and shut the door and pray to your Father who is in secret'. Prayer was never intended to be an act whereby one reveals their piety before others. This was something the Pharisees loved to do. In the silent place we are able to simply 'be' with God not distracted by our surroundings or the presence of others so that we can focus upon and listen to God. Solitude is the place where we can risk being transparent before God. He knows our heart, and it is important if we want to develop an intimate relationship with him that we be totally honest with him and with our self. We will only risk doing this when we are in the presence of one who loves and accepts us as we are unconditionally.

EXERCISE:

1. Go to a quiet place where you will not be disturbed for 30 minutes.

2. Read. Matt. 6:6-15.

3. In silence wait upon God. As thoughts enter your mind offer them in a prayer to God. Be careful not to avoid painful or disturbing ideas. This is a place where you can be open and vulnerable with God.

4. At the end of your prayer, conclude with the prayer Jesus taught in Matt.6:9-13.

DAY 7. TO PREPARE FOR ONES DEATH

DAY 7

Developing the discipline of silence and solitude as a mean of preparation for dying seems rather strange if not morbid. Yet dying, a reality that will happen to all of us, is something we need to face.

It is fascinating to understand that when people are dying they desire to have others with them, they do not want to go through the experience alone. Part of this can be explained by the fact we develop emotional bonds with people we love. They have become a part of our life and dying means there will be a separation of theses relationships. So at the time of death many experience 'separation anxiety'. They are afraid to let go, because they do not know what life will be like without the other.

I was with my youngest brother when he died. Quite suddenly he became very ill and was taken to the critical care unit at the local hospital. In the middle of the night I was called by the hospital staff to come and be with him because he had taken a turn for the worse and was not expected to live through the night. In that hospital room my parents, my wife and I gathered to be with him as he was dying. He was surrounded by people who loved and cared for him. We talked to him, we prayed with him and we held his hand. In that moment I wondered 'what is it like to die'? Regardless of the fact that he was surrounded by those who loved and cared for him, he still had to die by himself. What was he thinking? What was he feeling? What was this dying experience like?

As Christians we are given the promise of Jesus 'I will never leave you nor forsake you".
It suddenly became evident that as I learned to experience, and not just theorize about the

presence of Christ in my life, I would be able to face my own dying without anxiety and fear because I would know the awareness of Christ's presence in my day to day living. I would be able to identify with the Psalmist who said 'Even though I walk through the valley of the shadow of death, I will fear no evil for you are with me'. Ps.23:4.

There are different places in life where we are forced to be alone. It may be through sickness, times of forced confinement, and even death. All of these are places where no one else can enter with us. How we cope in these situations will depend upon our preparation. Learning the discipline of silence and solitude is part of that preparation.

EXERCISE:

1. Take an extended period to enter into silence. What is it like for you with no one around? What are the thoughts that keep coming to the forefront of your mind? What does this reveal to you?

2. Read Ps. 23. How do you identify with the writer? What comfort does the text give you as you face the challenges of your life?

3. In what way do you 'experience' the presence of Christ? Is this more than a theological concept? Explain.

4. Take some time to think about your own death. How will you experience the presence of Christ with you?

5. Write out your fears, anxieties and concerns about dying. Now write out a prayer and offer this to God.

6. Meditate on Romans 14:7-8

   "No one of us lives and equally no one of us dies, for himself alone. If we live we live unto the Lord; and if we die we die unto the Lord. Whether therefore we live or die, we belong to the Lord."

7. Memorize the following question and answer from the Heidelberg Catechism Q and A 1

Q. "What is your only comfort in life and in death?"

A. "That I am not my own, but belong - body and soul, in life and in death - to my faithful Saviour Jesus Christ".

Endnotes:

1.Robert Webber, Vickey Tusken, John Witvliet, Jack Schrader Renew! Songs and Hymns of Blended Worship. (Carol Stream: Hope Publishing Company) 1998 pg.10

2.C. S. Lewis www.opusangelorum.org/Formation/Silence and Solitude.pg.3 June 2000

3.Henri Nouwen, The Way of the Heart (New York: Ballantine Books) 1981 pg.13-15

4.Henri Nouwen, Genesee Dairy (New York: Double Day) 1976 pg. 148

5. John Ortburg, The Life You Always Wanted (Grand Rapids: Zondervan) 2003 pg. 82

6. Weavings December 1996 pg.40

7. Henri Nouwen, In the Name of Jesus (New Jersey: Crossroads) 1996 pg 18

8. ibid. pg. 22

9. ibid. pg. 38

10. ibid. pg. 39

11. ibid. pg 57-60

HOLY READING

The Bible has always played an important part in the spiritual formation of God's people since it is the word of God given to shape and direct our life.

There are many different ways to study the bible, but an ancient method called 'lectio divina', which can be translated 'holy reading' or 'sacred reading' dating back to the fourth century, is being rediscovered today.

In the Enlightenment era, there was a great emphasis upon understanding the text. Thus critical methodologies of studying the Bible were utilized. Today in the post-modern era there is a desire to understand the Bible in a holistic manner. Many are asking the question how does the biblical text speak to me as a person? Holy reading is a contemplative approach which helps us to hear the word of God as we read the text, and through this approach we discover an increasing ability to respond to what God has said to us through the text by offering more of ourselves and our relationships to God. In fact holy reading is a form of prayer. God speaks to us through scripture and then we speak back to God. This involves a shift from a typical approach to prayer where we begin by speaking to God and then conclude by saying 'amen'. We never remain silent long enough to allow God to speak into our lives, let alone accord him the honour of speaking to us first.

The Process:

The process of holy reading consists of a four-part movement, whereby we begin by reading the text and ultimately conclude with prayer. The four movements are:

1. LECTIO: (READING/LISTENING)

The practice of holy reading begins by developing the ability to listen and to hear what God is saying to us as we read the scriptures. In some respects we are like Elijah listening for the still small voice of God (I Kings 19:12).If we desire to hear the still small voice of God we must learn to be silent. If we are constantly speaking or if we are surrounded by noise and other distractions,we cannot hear the voice of God. The practice of holy reading therefore, requires that we become quiet in order to hear God's speaking to us through scripture.

Once you are quiet and still, read a short passage of scripture, and as you are reading listen for a word, phrase or concept that captures your attention. This is quite different from the way most of us read a book or the newspaper; often we try to take in a significant amount of content. Holy reading requires reverential listening; slowing down the pace, and listening in silence and with awe, for we are seeking to hear a word from God that will speak to our life situation.

2. MEDITATIO: (MEDITATION)

The second movement in holy reading is meditation. Having read the text and listening for a word or a phrase or a concept that speaks to us in a personal way; we meditate upon it. Meditation is more than simply thinking about an idea. A pastoral image of meditation is a picture of a cow lying in the field on a sunny day quietly chewing its cud, this is not far from what it is like to mull over the Word of God.

Jesus' mother Mary gives us an example of meditation. After Jesus birth she and Joseph were met by the shepherds who told them what the angel of the Lord had declared to them: "Do not be afraid. I bring you good news of great joy that will be for all the people. Today in the town of David a Saviour has been born to you; he is Christ the Lord." (Luke.2:10-11). When the shepherds left we are told Mary "treasured up all these things and pondered them in her heart". (Luke 2:19). In other words she thought about what they said and considered the impli-cations for her life, the life of her baby and ultimately the world at large. This illustration teaches us that meditation involves taking the Word of God and allowing it to interact with our thoughts, our hopes and our desires. It is through meditation we allow God's Word to become his word for us, a word that speaks to us at our deepest levels.

3. ORATIO (PRAYER)

The third movement in holy reading is prayer. God has spoken to us through his Word, we have meditated upon what he said, and now we speak back to God in prayer. This reinforces the concept that prayer is a dialogue. God speaks to us and then we speak to God. The prayer offered to God will be different for each individual. God will address various issues in each person's life simply because we are at different places and in different seasons of life. Therefore you might thank God for some insight He has given to you, or you might ask God for guidance or to give you a new perspective, or you might seek God's forgiveness, or you might enter into praise and adoration for who He is and what He has done. Through holy reading one discovers that God's word speaks powerfully into many different situations, and out of that place we speak back to God in a personal way.

4. CONTEMPLATIO (CONTEMPLATION)

In the final movement of holy reading we simply rest in the presence of God who has used his word as a means of inviting us to experience his embrace on our life. At this stage there is no agenda, you have come quietly into the presence of God, you have read his word, you have meditated upon it and as God has spoken to you, you speak back to him. Now you simply rest in his presence. You simply enjoy the experience of being in the presence of God. Many find this to be the most difficult stage or phase of holy reading. We are not used to being silent and simply resting in God. We are activists. In fact it is not surprising that in this stage many will find their mind begins to wonder. If this occurs simply re-read the passage or go back to the word, phrase or concept that God has spoken to you, continue to meditate upon it and then allow yourself to be in the presence of God.

THE PRACTICE OF HOLY READING

Choose a text that you desire to meditate on. Some will be working through a book of the Bible; others might be working through passages based on a thematic approach.

Before you begin to read the text you need to take some time to become quiet. Make sure there are no distractions or interruptions for the next few minutes. Find a comfortable position and quiet yourself down. Begin with a short prayer inviting the Lord to speak into your life.

Take the text you have chosen for the day and read it slowly. It is helpful to read out loud as this not only slows down the reading process but it also helps you understand and appreciate the emotional tone of the text. As you read the text listen for a word, phrase or an idea that speaks to you. Then sit in silence for two or three minutes.

When a word or phrase comes to mind, slowly repeat it to yourself and allow it to interact with your own thoughts and ideas. Allow this meditation to lead you into a deeper dialogue with God.

In your dialogue with God speak to him even as he has spoken to you. In other words you give to him what you have discovered during your experience of meditation. This is the basis of your prayer. But allow your prayer to come from the depth of your heart and be careful not to intellectualize this experience.

Finally you rest in God. You enter into the presence of God and simply wait. This is a state of being not a state of doing, whereby we simply enjoy God.

PRACTICAL SUGGESTIONS

Ken Boa has offered some very helpful and practical suggestions to enable each participant in holy reading to move through the four stages with relative ease.[1]

LECTIO:

* Choose a place that is inviting and where you will not be distracted.
* Be systematic in your reading. Some will work through an entire book, while others will use the lectionary as a guide.
* Avoid using a bible with study notes. These notes tend to be distracting.
* Do not read long passages of scripture. In your reading you want to read slowly

and repeatedly as you allow the word of God to move into the depth of your being.
* *Remember, in lectio you are seeking to be 'shaped by the word of God' rather than just 'gaining information about the word of God'.*

MEDATIO:

* *Read the text slowly; remember you are not in a rush.*
* *Try to engage as much as possible your five senses as you meditate upon the text. Some passages in the Bible enable this process more readily than others. For example Psalm 1 speaks about one who mediates upon the word of God and compares the outcome to a tree planted by rivers of water. It is quite easy to see this picture.*
* *Some find it helpful to keep a journal and to write down their thoughts. During meditation this has two benefits. First it helps to keep your mind from wandering, and second it enables you to come back to the text at a later date and re-read what God was saying to you in the process.*
* *Continue to practice meditation; it is not a one off experience. As you become more familiar with this discipline you will discover great benefits.*

ORATIO:

* *Take time to pray. Many are intrigued by the reading but do not leave enough time to pray.*
* *As God has spoken to you through the scriptures your prayer will be in response to what God has said. Thus the prayer will differ according to the work of God's spirit. The prayer may be one of confession, or thanksgiving, or petition or adoration.*
* *In your prayer speak as one who speaks to a friend.*

CONTEMPLATIO:

* *Don't be concerned about what to do. Simply rest in the presence of God.*
* *Try to recall what God has spoken into your heart during the meditation and repeat this to yourself.*
* *If you are an extrovert recognize this is going to be a stretch for you. Keep at it.*

THE PROCESS OF GROUP LECTIO

This is a basic outline of 'holy reading' you may choose to use in a group setting. In this context there will be an appointed reader who will read the passage for the group and who will instruct the group when to move at the appropriate time to the next step in the process. The reader should try to participate as fully as possible in the exercise although this may be a bit difficult for a novice leader.

1. LISTEN TO THE WORD OF GOD

1. Prepare yourself by sitting in silence for a few minutes

2. Read the passage out loud

3. Listen for a word or phrase that catches your attention

4. Say the word over and over in your mind.

5. Remain silent for 2-3 minutes following the reading.

2. ASK: "HOW IS MY LIFE TOUCHED BY THIS WORD OF GOD?"

1. Read the passage a second time.

2. After the reading sit in silence and meditate upon this question.

3. After 2-3 minutes of silence go around the group and briefly share the connection between the phrase or word and their life.

3. ASK: "WHAT DOES GOD WANT ME TO DO?"

1. Read the passage a third time.

2. After the reading sit in silence and meditate upon the question.

3. After 2-3 minutes of silence go around the group and briefly share what you think God wants you to do in response.

4. PRAY FOR EACH OTHER TO BE ABLE TO RESPOND TO GOD'S INVITATION

1. Pray for the person beside you.

2. Pray according to what God has spoken into their life.

5. REST IN GOD

1. When everyone has prayed the group enters a time if silence just to savour what God has done and to enjoy His presence. Resist the desire to talk.

2. After an appropriate time of silence the leader will offer a closing prayer.

EXERCISES:

This week there will be an opportunity to spend fifteen to thirty minutes a day in holy reading. It is important to remember that this discipline is learned by repetition; therefore you are encouraged to do this on a regular basis.

The following guidelines are offered to assist you in this exercise if you are doing it on your own.

1. Preparation: You need to prepare for this exercise by sitting quietly and offering this time to God. Invite the Lord into this place and ask him to make himself known to you through his word.

2. Reading: Read the text out loud and listen for a word or an idea that resonates with you. Say it over and over in your mind or out loud.

3. Meditation: When a word or phrase resonates with you turn it over and over in your mind. How does it speak into your life?

4. Pray: As God speaks to you through the scripture pray this back to Him. Do not censor your prayer, that is, speaking what you think God would want you to say rather than speaking what is in your heart. Speak plainly and directly from your heart.

5. Contemplate: When you have completed the prayer sit silently before God. Enjoy His presence and rest in Him.

6. Journal: When you have completed the period of contemplation write in your journal any thoughts that you need to keep as a reminder of God's word to you. Offer a prayer of thanksgiving as you leave this space.

SECURITY IN MY RELATIONSHIP WITH GOD

DAY 1: JOHN 10:7-15

What truth did God speak into your life today?

DAY 2. LUKE 15:1-7

What truth did God speak into your life today?

DAY 3. PHILIPPIANS 1:3-11

What truth did God speak into your life today?

DAY 4. ISAIAH 43: 1-6

What truth did God speak into your life today?

DAY 5. JEREMIAH 29:11-14

What truth did God speak into your life today?

DAY 6. PS.27:1-14

What truth did God speak into your life today?

DAY 7. PS. 121:1-8

What truth did God speak into your life today?

At the end of this week review all the statements you have written and then write a prayer of thanksgiving to God for reassuring you of the security you have in your relationship with him.

PRAYER:

Endnotes:

1. Kenneth Boa, Conformed to His Image (Grand Rapids Michigan; Zondervan) 2001 pg.174-183.

PRAYING THE SCRIPTURES

In prayer we are seeking to deepen our relationship with God so that we are aware of his continual presence and sensitive to his working in and though our lives.

However there are those who find prayer not only difficult but also routine, somewhat repetitive and at times boring. Ken Boa states: "The problem with prayer is heightened by the fact that people often succumb either to the extreme of all form and no freedom, or the opposite extreme of all freedom and no form. The first extreme leads to a rote or impersonal approach to prayer, while the second produces an unbalanced and undisciplined prayer life that can degenerate into a litany of one 'gimmie' after another". [1]

Some view prayer as simply talking to God and have learned to pray by reciting what might be termed 'formula prayers'. Many can recall the well known evening prayer "Now I lay me down to sleep, I pray the Lord my soul to keep. If I should die before I wake, I pray the Lord my soul to take". There are other 'formula prayers' more profound and thoughtful such as the prayer Jesus taught, commonly referred to as 'The Lord's Prayer'. In addition there are many helpful prayers found in various 'Prayer Books'. These prayers are valuable and valid forms of prayer which sustained people throughout the years and helped them to deepen their relationship with God.

However if one prays these prayers in a mechanical manner with little attention to what is being said, they become a monologue instead of a heartfelt conversation with God. At this point these prayers have lost touch with the immediacy of personal experience with God and what was once a meaningful expression of a genuine spiritual experience is now a prayer totally detached from life. The prayer is not a response to the presence of God but simply an exercise to be done. If this is our approach to prayer, it is no wonder that our prayer life is routine, repetitive and boring.

In contrast to the 'formula prayer' is the 'extemporaneous prayer'. Many who come to faith in later years not having being taught to pray in childhood; frequently learn the discipline of prayer by listening to their pastor lead the congregational prayers. If they follow this format without making it their own, they discover they are simply repeating the same prayers day after day and they too have fallen into a similar pattern as those who are taught 'formula prayers'. 'Extemporaneous prayers' are based on a formula. If you don't believe this listen to people pray in an extemporaneous fashion and note the phrases and terminology that are used over and over again. The main difference between 'formula prayer' and 'extemporaneous prayer' is that 'extemporaneous prayers' are not expressed as clearly, concisely and thoughtfully. The other factor that seems to be evident in most 'extemporaneous prayer' is the person praying tends to focus on petition. In other words we continuously ask God to meet our needs. This is not wrong; in fact the Bible encourages us to do so. However if this is the focal point of our prayers, we need to realize something is lacking in our relationship with God.

In order to deepen our relationship with God and to find a more comprehensive manner of praying, it is helpful to learn to pray the scriptures. Before we begin with some practical aspects of this approach to prayer, we need to understand that if we desire to deepen our relationship with God it does not necessarily depend upon spending long hours in prayer, although that might eventually develop. We begin by developing a more contemplative attitude. Gula states: "with Scripture we can take a long loving look at God's actions toward us; we can look at Jesus and become absorbed in what he is like, what he says, what he does, what he cares about. Scripture is a privileged place where we go to put ourselves more explicitly in the Lord's presence. If the goal of our spiritual striving is to know the Lord God, to become more deeply in love with God, and to be alive in the Spirit (in short to be a disciple of Jesus) then Scripture is a special encounter for our heartfelt knowledge and personal relationship with God to grow.

In Scripture we find expressions of God's deepest desires for us, of God's attitude toward us, and of God's willingness to be involved with us. The directness of the biblical word's expression of God's desire to be in a loving relationship with us calls for a response. We react to the biblical word in a way we would to any provocative statement addressed to us. If we like what we hear, we respond with approval and enthusiasm; if we do not like it, we want to stop listening and turn from it. What we cannot avoid is that the bible expresses the word of the living God who wants to engage in dialogue with us. So we need to approach the Bible in prayer as a word addressed to us personally calling for a response. "What do I hear the Lord saying to me?" is the fundamental question we bring to scripture when we pray".[2]

As we read the scripture we need to ask "am I attentively present to God?" Being attentive takes effort, it does not just happen. When we pay attention, we have to stop being preoccupied with ourselves and make the effort to be fully present with the other. If you struggle with this practice try the following exercises. Listen to some music, read a book or go for a walk and be observant of nature. All these activities are acts of paying attention, and as you think about what you read or hear or see you are becoming contemplative. This contemplative attitude is what we need to bring as we read scripture and pray.

To pray the scriptures is the practice of using God's word as the foundation for shaping our prayers, for communion with him, and intercession for others. It is speaking with God in his own words. Scripture praying is putting an equal emphasis upon the Word of God and prayer; it is the realization that prayer is a dialogue between us and God. We might read one of Paul's prayers for the early Christians and make it a prayer of thanksgiving, or sing a psalm of praise, or meditate upon a story in the gospel which has a focus upon forgiveness. In each of these instances the particular text chosen and the place where we find ourselves at the moment will influence and structure the prayer.

There are times when we discover we do not have the words to adequately express our thoughts, feelings or emotions, but as we pray the scriptures we find expression though the Word of God. When we allow God's word to be the expression of our prayers, it is capable of declaring deep inner desires and thoughts.

Every day when rising to greet the day and when preparing to rest at night, Jesus, like all devout Jews would pray the Shema "Hear O Israel: the Lord our God is one. Love the Lord your God with all your heart and with all your soul and with all your strength." (Deuteronomy 6:4-5). He would also recite this prayer at the beginning of every service in the synagogue. In addition to praying the Shema, Jesus would regularly pray the Psalms. When dying on the cross the prayer he prayed was one he learned as a child, but in this instance it took on new meaning "My God, my God, why have you forsaken me?" (Psalm 22:1).

In the Bible there are many examples of recorded prayers. Abraham's servant as he is seeking for the right wife for his master's son Isaac prays: "O Lord God of my master Abraham, give me success today, and show kindness to my master Abraham. See I am standing beside this spring, and the daughters of the townspeople are coming to draw water. May it be that when I say to a girl, 'Please let down your jar that I may have a drink,' and if she says, 'Drink and I'll water your camels too'- let her be the one you have chosen for your servant Isaac. By this I will know that you have shown kindness to my master." (Genesis 24:12-14)

When Nehemiah heard the city of Jerusalem was in ruins he sat down, wept, mourned and prayed. "O Lord God of heaven the great and awesome God, who keeps his covenant of love with those who love him and obey his commandments, let your ear be attentive and your eyes open to hear the prayer your servant is praying before you day and night for your servants, the people of Israel. I confess the sins we Israelites, including myself and my father's house have committed against you. We have acted very wickedly toward you. We have not obeyed the commands, decrees and laws you gave your servant Moses.

Remember the instruction you gave your servant Moses, saying, 'If you are unfaithful I will scatter you among the nations, but if you return to me and obey my commands, then even if your exiled people are at the farthest horizon, I will gather them from that place and bring them to the place I have chosen as a dwelling place for my name.

"They are your servants and your people, whom you redeemed by your great strength and your mighty hand. O Lord let your ear be attentive to the prayer of this your servant and to the prayer of your servants who delight in revering your name. Give your servant success today by granting him favour in the presence of this man." (Nehemiah 1:8-11)

The Apostle Paul prays that the Christians in Ephesus would know and experience all they have in Christ. "I pray that out of his glorious riches he may strengthen you with power through his Spirit in your inner being, so that Christ may dwell in your hearts through faith. And I pray that you, being rooted and established in love, may have power, together with all the saints to grasp how long and wide and high and deep is the love of Christ, and to know this love that surpasses knowledge-that you may be filled to the measure of all the fullness of God.

Now to him who is able to do immeasurably more than all we ask or imagine, according to his power that is at work within us, to him be glory in the church and in Christ Jesus through all generations, forever and ever! Amen." (Ephesians 3:14-21)

As we read these prayers we gain insight into the life of the person who expressed the prayer. But in addition we can make these prayers our own, as we identify with them. For example we may pray for people in our community of faith and these prayers might simply be 'Lord, I ask you to bless these people in all they do this day'. To be honest this prayer does sound rather trite! How enriching it is to pray as Paul did for the church at Ephesus. To paraphrase his prayer (Ephesians 3:14-19) we might pray 'Lord may these people know the full extent of your love for them. It is beyond our ability to fully comprehend what all this means yet we know it can be experienced in our lives. Knowing who you are and what you can do, we live with confidence you are able to do this. Amen'.

In this manner we are praying Scripture.

PRACTICAL GUIDELINES IN PRAYING THE SCRIPTURES:

1. Read the Passage:

As you begin this process read the text slowly and out loud. When you do this you will discover you do not read as quickly, you are not easily distracted and you will find you read with a greater awareness of the emotion(s) expressed in the passage. Do not rush through the reading. Think about words or phrases or ideas that capture your attention and listen to the way God is speaking to you through the text.

Having read the passage, write out from memory words, phrases or ideas that seem to speak to you. Explore what these words mean to you and what God may be saying to you from his word that speaks into your world, your life, your self.

2. You might choose to rewrite the passage in your own words. This can become part of your prayer as you speak back to God what he has spoken to you.

3. At times you will receive great insight and at other times there seems to be nothing. Remember this is not an exercise you attempt to 'get through; it is a place to find God. You might need to come back to a passage several times until you are satisfied that the message has sunk into your life.

EXERCISES

The following exercise are intended to allow you to experience praying with Scripture over a period of seven days and each day will focus upon a specific type of prayer.

DAY 1. PRAYING THE PSALMS

Today we will focus on praying a psalm. The psalms are a wonderful resource for prayer because they address all aspects of the human condition as well as the moods we experience as a result of life's experiences. At times there will be deep sadness and at other times there will be shouts of joy.

The Psalms are also intended to be sung. As we sing our emotions are awakened and in all probability some will find this a challenge especially of we are accustomed to keeping them in check. St. Augustine said: "he who sings prays twice". In other words we not only articulate words through the song but as we sing our emotions are deeply stirred as well.

DAY
1

1. Read Psalm 23. Read the passage slowly and savour words or phrases that speak to you.

<blockquote>
The Lord is my shepherd I shall not want.

He makes me lie down in green pastures,

He leads me beside quiet waters,

He restores my soul.

He guides me in paths of righteousness

For his names sake.

Even though I walk through the valley of the shadow of death,

I will fear no evil,

For you are with me;

Your rod and staff they comfort me.

You prepare a table before me

In the presence of my enemies.

You anoint my head with oil; my cup overflows.

Surely goodness and mercy will follow me all the days of my life

And I will dwell in the house of the lord

Forever.
</blockquote>

2. List some of the images in the Psalm that you find significant. Why are they so powerful in your life? What might God be saying to you?

3. Sing this psalm out loud. There are various hymn books with musical scores to enable you to sing this scripture. What do you experience as you sing?

4. Pray this Psalm back to God. Use language that you are comfortable with and try to avoid clichés.

DAY 2

DAY 2. VENGEANCE

There is another type of prayer most are reticent to pray, it is one that speaks of vengeance or getting even. These are known as the imprecatory psalms.

<blockquote>
Rise up, O Lord!

Deliver me, O my God!

For you strike all my enemies on the cheek;

You break the teeth of the wicked. (Psalm 3:7)
</blockquote>

As we read these words most of us cringe. It is not that we have never given this a thought, but somehow it does not seem to be an attitude we should have as followers of Jesus. At the very least we must acknowledge these psalms are realistic in that they portray the emotions we experience as a result of injustices. In fact some of the most powerful human emotions are those of revenge and retaliation. When we have been hurt or injured we want to 'get even'. When we pray prayers, such as Psalm 3:7 there are definitely some benefits. Bruggemann states when we pray in this manner it is certainly a cathartic experience and it serves to "legitimate and affirm these most intense elements of rage".[3]

As you pray these psalms it is important to understand the words of vengeance are offered to God. Bruggemann states: "When vengeance is entrusted to God, the speaker is relatively free from its power. The speaker, with all the hurt and joy, affirms himself or herself to be God's creature. That recognition of being in God's realm and able to address God gives perspective to the venom.' [4]

The Bible teaches vengeance belongs to God and not to us. The Apostle Paul writes "Do not take revenge, my friends, but leave room for God's wrath, for it is written: 'It is mine to avenge; I will repay,' says the Lord." (Romans 12:19) The writer to the Hebrews declares" It is mine to avenge I will repay…The Lord will judge his people." (Hebrews 10:30). With this in mind we never need to retaliate even though we may desire to do so. However it is only as we honestly pray these prayers will we be able to come to the place where we can release our emotions, experience God's healing grace and then be in the place where we can honestly 'love our enemies and pray for those who persecute us.' (Matthew 5:43-48)

Psalms 5, 6, 11, 12, 35, 37, 40, 52, 54, 56, 58,69, 79, 83, 109,137, 139, and 143 are the Imprecatory Psalms

1. Choose one of these Psalms and read it out loud.

2. As you read, note the emotions that begin to rise within you. How do you perceive this to be related to some experience in your life? Does some memory come flooding back into your conscious awareness?

3. Slowly pray this Psalm to God. As you do, offer to him the hurt you have experienced, aware that vengeance is not an option for you. You must choose to leave any act of vengeance with God.

4. Read Romans 12:14-21

5. Write out your own Imprecatory psalm.

DAY 3

6. What is it like to express this type of prayer? What have you learned about God? Yourself? Your enemy?

7. How do you integrate praying this type of psalm with the concept of forgiveness?

DAY 3. MEDITATION

Meditation is a wonderful way to appropriate the Word of God and to apply it to life. In Eastern religions, meditation is used as one aspect of attaining 'enlightenment'. Christian meditation is rooted and grounded in the Scriptures and involves a pondering and reflecting upon the word of God. In fact the bible commands us to meditate. The psalmist declares "his delight is in the law of the Lord and in His law he meditates day and night' (Psalm 1:2). God told Joshua "Do not let this Book of the Law depart from your mouth. Meditate on it day and night, so that you may be careful to do everything written in it. Then you will be prosperous and successful in all you do."(Joshua 1:8)

Years ago George Muller wrote about the significance of meditation.

"Now I saw that the most important thing was to give myself to the reading of God's Word, and to meditation on it, that thus my heart might be comforted, encouraged, warmed, reproved, instructed, and that thus, by means of the Word of God, whilst meditating on it, my heart might be brought into experiential communion with the Lord…. Now what is food for the inner man? Not prayer, but the Word of God; and here again, not the simple reading of the Word of God, so that it passes through our minds, just as water passes through a pipe, but considering what we read, pondering over it and applying it to our hearts".[5]

Tan and Gregg define meditation as "pondering over scripture passages in such a way that the written Word of God becomes a living Word of God applied to our hearts by the Holy Spirit…. Meditation is the process of thinking through language that takes place in the heart or inner life. The truth being meditated upon moves from the heart to the mouth, (murmuring) to the mind, (reflective thinking) and finally to the heart (outer action). The person meditating seeks to understand how to relate biblical truth to life".[6]

Meditation helps us enter into the scripture story using as many of the five senses as possible. By this process we become active participants rather than passive observers. Some object to this approach since it is highly subjective and there is the possibility one could be deceived by the enemy. This is true and caution must be exercised. However Jesus used imagination when he taught. For example he told a story of a farmer who went out to sow seed. Some fell on hard soil, some on shallow ground, some was mixed with weeds and some fell on fertile ground. It is very easy for a reader to see what Jesus was trying to communicate; you can visualize the story, you can smell the earth and feel the intensity of the sun as it beats upon you. When we meditate on scripture and use our senses in trying to fully appropriate the Word of God, we need to pray that God will sanctify our imagination even as he does our reason, so we will grasp the truth of what he is saying.

GUIDELINES FOR MEDITATING

Preparation:
Relax in a quiet setting. For some this may be a special room in the house, or sitting in a park or resting in a church sanctuary. Whatever place you choose it needs to be inviting and not distracting.

Be aware of your body. Are you tense, anxious or relaxed? Have you come from an event that has left you breathless? What is your body telling you? If you are feeling tired it will be difficult to enter into meditation because you will fall asleep.

Some find it helpful to play quiet instrumental music in the background. This should not be a distraction but an aid to becoming 'centred' and 'focused'.

1. *Begin your meditation by sitting silently before God. Become aware of God's presence with you. If your mind is racing or filled with various thoughts that cause you concern or distress give that over to God. Allow him to bring his peace into your life.*

2. *Begin with a prayer: Ask God to be present, to teach you, to protect you from deception and to guide you through this meditation.*

3. *Choose a story. Read it over a few times so that you have a sense of the story and if possible try to visualize what you are reading. As you read the story picture what is happening. You might find yourself identifying with one of the characters. If this happens try to explore what you are feeling and experiencing.*

4. *Read Isaiah 53:1-12.*

5. *Write down what you have heard from God or what you have learned from this meditation.*

6. *Following the meditation, use this passage as the basis of your prayer. Write out your prayer and when you have finished re-read it. Do you discover any significant truths?*

7. As you leave your meditation try to return to it several times throughout the day. Discover how God will use his word to speak into the situations you encounter in the day.

8. In this process of meditation remember that you can't be in a rush.

DAY 4. INTERCESSION

DAY
4

A great portion of our prayers and those written in the Scriptures are based upon intercession and petition. By examining them we gain insight into the requests made by the authors of scripture and these examples of prayer encourage us in making our petitions to God.

In this exercise we do not simply read the prayer we make it our own. In other words we contextualize the prayer.

In the prayer today you may choose one of several different texts. The text you choose may depend upon your circumstances, for example you may be seeking insight or answers to a particular problem you are encountering.

- Praying for safety. (Genesis32:9-12)
- Praying for a child. (1Samuel 1:9-18)
- Asking God for healing. (Mark 9: 17-24)
- Praying for unity in the church. (Romans 15: 5-6)
- A prayer of blessing. (Numbers 6:22-27)
- Asking for wisdom. (2 Chronicles 1:7-13)
- Praying for descendants. (1Chronicles 17:16-27)

1. Read the passage you have chosen.

2. Allow yourself to see this prayer in the light of your own story.

3. Pray this text to God.

PRAYER FOR PEACE

Lord, make me an instrument of your peace,
Where there is hatred, let me sow love;
Where there is injury, pardon;
Where there is doubt, faith;
Where there is despair, hope;
Where there is darkness, light;
Where there is sadness, joy.

O Divine Master, grant that I may seek not so
Much to be consoled as to console;
To be understood, as to understand,
To be loved, as to love;
For it is in giving that we receive,
It is in pardoning we are pardoned,
And it is in dying that we are born to
Eternal life.

(Francis of Assisi)

SEEKING DIRECTION

Lord Jesus Christ,
You are the light of the world;
Light up our lives when we are in darkness.

In the darkness of our uncertainty –
When we don't know what to do,
When decisions are hard top take;
Lord give us light to guide us.

In the darkness of our anxiety –
When we are worried about what the future may bring,
When we don't know where to turn:
Lord, give us the light of your peace.

In the darkness of our despair –
When life seems empty,
When we feel there is not point in going on:
Lord give us the light of your hope
Amen
(Adapted from Contemporary Prayers)

DAY 5

DAY 5. JUSTICE AND COMPASSION

Two important characteristics of God are those of justice and compassion. When we think of the word justice some might see an image of a stern judge and solemn jury. There is also the notion of balance, such as Lady Justice who is blindfolded and balances scales according to the impartial requirements of the law. Justice is perceived to be impartial to people and stands above any special pleadings. We have come to expect God as the judge who at the end of time will separate the good from the bad according to the requirements of his commandments.

On the other hand when we think of compassion we think about acts such as feeding the hungry, caring for the sick or extending forgiveness when wronged. In the gospels we see many instances when Jesus demonstrated compassion toward people, not only in what he said but also in what he did.

The biblical understanding of justice comes from Israel's experience with God. In this relationship they discovered that God's justice was extremely generous. From the call of Abram to the liberation of the Israelites from Egypt, to the entering the Promised Land, Israel has no claim or right to what God gives. However God's justice reveals the greatness and kindness of the Lord.

As we experience the generosity of God we are to be generous toward one another. When we encounter those in need, or suffering, we are to do all we can to help them. In doing this we are accomplishing the justice and compassion of God.

Because of sin this requirement of justice is not always realized. In the Old Testament God raised up prophets to announce to the people, the need for justice and compassion. Amos made this the focal point of his preaching. He declared that there can be no right relationship with God if the requirements of justice are ignored.

Isaiah told the people that even if they had the correct form of worship and offered sacrifices to God; their offerings would not be accepted if they did not treat the people with justice.

In the New Testament we see justice and compassion joined together. We are never so just as when we love; when we seek the good of the other. The Apostle Paul stated we are to owe no debt except the debt of love. Love and justice come together when we respond to the neighbour who needs us here and now. This is a fundamental spirituality for one who is a follower of Jesus.

He has shown you O man,
What is good?
And what does the Lord
Require of you?
To act justly and to love
Mercy
And to walk humbly with
Your God.
(Micah 6:8)

The prophets call us to see and hear what we often miss on our own. At times we have become indifferent to the needs and issues of our day. Micah as all the other prophets, is concerned we do not fall into the trap of being religious but not having a heart that reflects the heart of God. Three words stand out; justice, kindness, humility. Take some time in self examination to see if this is a reality in your life.

EXERCISE:

Read Isaiah 58. Note the requirements of a true spiritual fast.

Take some time in personal reflection. Ask probing questions about your spiritual life. To what extent do I show justice and compassion to others? Am I concerned about the poor and the marginalized? How do I actually reveal this?

Conclude with one of the following prayers:

O God,
Open our eyes that we may see the needs of others;
Open our ears that we may hear their cries;
Open our hearts that we may feel their anguish and their joy.
Let us not be afraid to defend the oppressed, the poor, the powerless, because of the anger and the might of the powerful.
Show us where love and hope and faith are needed, and use us to bring them to those places.
Open our ears and eyes, our hearts and lives that we may in these coming days be able to work for justice and peace with you.
Amen

-Anti Poverty Sunday Prayers. Micah Challenge Australia.

Thank you God for Jesus,
Who came
To seek and save the lost.
To set the captives free,
To feed the hungry,
To touch the sick with healing,
To love the unloved,
To speak out at injustice, to give life where there was death.

Help us Lord, to be like your son Jesus.
To see as he sees and to act on his word.
We ask for your help in these things.

Amen.

Prayers for Justice www.cuf.org.uk

Heavenly Father
You who are faithful and true and righteous in all you ways,
Teach us to choose what is right and stand against
That which is evil.
Teach us to love justice and mercy and stand against
Oppression and exploitation.
Show us where we are indifferent to these things.
Empower us with you spirit, so that we may have courage
And determination to do your will.

We trust you because you are Lord
And you love endures forever.

Amen.

Prayers for Justice www.cuf.org.uk

DAY 6. DOXOLOGY

DAY
6

A doxology is a hymn or expression of praise unto God. There are numerous examples of doxologies in the scriptures simply because there was the conviction that everything that exists and happens is for the purpose of drawing attention to God. Since the fourth century the most common doxology known as the 'Gloria Patri' or the 'Lesser Doxology' offered after the reading of the Psalms, declared "Glory be to the Father and to the Son and to the Holy Ghost. As it was in the beginning, is now, and ever shall be world without end .Amen".

Later in the fourth century there was the addition of the 'Greater Doxology' or the 'Gloria in Excelsis'. This description of praise was taken from the text Luke 2:14. "Glory to God in the highest, and on earth peace to men on whom his favour rests". When this doxology was incorporated into the Latin mass it was said at the beginning of the service. The Reformers, emulating the early church who concluded their worship by singing a song, sang the doxology at the conclusion of their service. The song we are most familiar with today as a doxology is:

Praise God from whom all blessings flow; praise him all creatures here below;
praise him above ye heavenly hosts; praise Father, Son and Holy Ghost. Amen.
(Thomas Kent) public domain

Biblical Doxologies

My soul magnifies the Lord and my spirit rejoices in God my Saviour.
(Luke 1:46-47)

Oh, the depth of the riches of the wisdom of God!
How unsearchable his judgments,
and his paths beyond tracing out!
Who has known the mind of the Lord?
Or who has been his counsellor?
Who has ever given to God,
that God should repay him?
For from him and through him and to him are all things.
To him be the glory forever and ever! (Romans 11:33-36)

To the King eternal, immortal, invisible, the only God, be honour
and glory forever and ever. (1Timothy 1:17)

Unto him who is the blessed and only potentate, the King of kings and Lord of lords; who only hath immortality, dwelling in the light which no one can approach unto; whom no one has seen, nor can see; be honour and power everlasting.
(1 Timothy 6:15-16)

Now unto him that is able to keep you from falling and to present you faultless before the presence of his glory with exceeding great joy, to the only wise God our Saviour, be glory and majesty, dominion and power, both now and ever.
(Jude 24-25)

To him who loves us and has set us free from our sins with his blood, who has made us a royal house to serve as the priests of his God and Father - to him be glory and dominion for ever! (Revelation 1:5-6)

Holy, holy, holy is the Lord God Almighty, who was, who is, and who is to come.
(Revelation 4:8)

You are worthy, our Lord and God, to receive glory and honour and power, for you created all things, and by your will they were created and have their being.
(Revelation 4:11)

Blessing and glory and wisdom and thanksgiving and honour and power and might be to our God forever and ever! (Revelation 7:12)

EXERCISE:

1. Read Romans 11. As you come to the end of this chapter you will note the doxology which is the climax of all Paul has been trying to express.

2. Choose one doxology from the list and read it several times during the day? What do you learn from this experience? Write your response in your journal?

3. How can doxology enhance your relationship with God?

DAY 7. BLESSING AND BENEDICTION:

DAY
7

In the scriptures prayers of blessing or benediction are often spoken over individuals or congregations. In speaking a blessing the person does more than just recite familiar words, rather they are asking for God's favour to rest upon the recipient.

When Jacob was dying he gathered his sons around him and blessed each one in an appropriate manner. (Genesis 49:28) Before the nation of Israel entered the Promised Land Moses blessed all the people. Although it is an extensive blessing he concluded with these words, "Blessed are you, O Israel! Who is like you a people saved by the Lord? He is your shield and helper and your glorious sword. Your enemies will cower before you, and you will trample down their high places." Dueteronomy 33:29.

There are several accounts of congregations being blessed by their spiritual leaders. When the Ark of the Covenant was returned to Zion, David "blessed the people in the name of the Lord" (2 Samuel 6:18). On another occasion the Levitical priests blessed the people during the observance of Passover (2 Chronicles 30: 27).

The Latin root of benediction means 'to speak well'. In one sense benedictions are quite prevalent in our day to day encounters. It is not uncommon to hear people say "have a good day" or "keep your hopes up". When we say goodbye we might offer the benediction "God be with you". However the secular benedictions (Hang Tough! Don't Give Up!) imply action on the part of the person to whom the blessing is extended as though that person was responsible for the outcome. Biblical benedictions are professions of faith that God is sovereign and responsible for the outcome. Benedictions such as "The Lord Bless You!" or "The Peace of God Be Upon You!" are expressions of grace. We do not bless ourselves, God blesses us. So when we offer a benediction to another we are acting in God's place, assuring them that God is for them.

There are numerous blessings in the scriptures which you are encouraged to learn and pray over individuals or congregations. In doing this you are praying God's best upon them.

> The Lord bless you and keep you;
> The Lord make his face to shine upon you and be gracious unto you;
> The Lord turn his face toward you and give you peace.
> Amen (Numbers 6:24-26)

This blessing contains five parts that help us understand the components of a blessing and what God will do.
a. Bless and keep. (favour and protect)
b. Make his face shine upon them. (be pleased)
c. Be gracious. (merciful and compassionate)
d. Turn his face toward them. (give his approval)
e. Give you peace. (sense of well being)

The peace of God which passes all understanding,
Keep your hearts and minds
In the knowledge and love of God,
And of God's Son Jesus Christ our Lord:
And the blessing of God almighty
The Father and the Son and the Holy Spirit,
Remain with you always.
Amen. (Philippians 4:7)

May the God of Peace
Make you holy in every way
And keep your whole being-
Spirit, soul and body-
Free from every fault
At the coming of our Lord Jesus Christ.
Amen. (1 Thessalonians 5:23)

May the God of hope
Fill you with all joy and peace in believing
So that by the power of the Holy Spirit
You may abound in hope.
Amen. (Romans 15:13)

Now may the God of peace
Who brought back from the dead our Lord Jesus,
The great shepherd of the sheep,
By the blood of the eternal covenant
Make you complete in everything good
So that you may do God's will,
Working among you
That which is pleasing in God's sight,
Through Jesus Christ,
To whom be glory forever and ever.
Amen
(adapted from Hebrews 13:20-21)

To him who is able to keep you from falling
And to present you before his glorious presence,
Without fault and with great joy-
To the only God our Saviour be glory, majesty, power and authority,
Through Jesus Christ our Lord,
Before all ages,
Now and forevermore!
Amen.
(Jude 24-25)

Exercise:

1. Memorize the Aaronic Blessing Numbers 6:24-26

2. At the conclusion of your daily prayer, take some time to personally meditate upon one of the blessings you have discovered in scripture. How will this blessing speak into your life on this day?

3. Seek an opportunity this week to offer a blessing to another, perhaps it will be a member of your family or to your congregation.

4. How can you take some of the 'secular blessings' (Have a Good Day! or Hang in There!) and turn these into a Christian blessing? Find opportunities to use these blessings in the ordinariness of your day.

Endnotes:

1. Ken Boa, Handbook to Prayer (Atlanta Georgia: Trinity House Publishing Co.) 1993. Pg.1
2. Richard Gula, Spirituality Today Winter 1984,vol.36, No.4, pp. 292-306
3. Bruggemann Walter Praying the Psalms (Winona Minn: St Mary's Press) 1993. pg.59
4. ibid., pg 60
5. Siang -Yang Tan, Douglas H. Gregg Disciplines of the Holy Spirit
   (Grand Rapids Michigan: Zondervan) 1997, pg. 86
6. ibid. pg.86.

CONFESSION

The need for **confession** as a **spiritual discipline** is based on the fact we have sinned against God and we **need His forgiveness.**

In a post modern culture some do not want to think about sin let alone mention it, and will go as far as to accuse Christians of being obsessed about sin. John Stott declares that Christians do talk about sin; in fact he says we talk about it a lot. Why do we do this? He states, "We do so for the simple reason that we are realists. Sin is an ugly fact. It is neither to be ignored nor ridiculed, but honestly faced. Indeed, Christianity is the only religion in the world which takes sin seriously and offers a satisfactory remedy for it. And the way to enjoy this remedy is not to deny it but to confess it". [1]

Maxie Dunnam states: "The witness of scripture is that the dominant desire in God's heart is the desire to forgive." [2]

The psalmist David experienced this in his life as we see in his prayer recorded in Psalm 51.

> Have mercy upon me, O God,
> According to your unfailing love;
> According to your great compassion
> Blot out my transgressions.
> Wash away all my iniquity
> And cleanse me from my sin.
>
> For I know my transgressions,
> And my sin is always before me.
> Against you, you will only, have I sinned
> And done and what is evil in your sight.
> So you are proved right when you speak

And justified when you judge.
Surely I have been a sinner from birth,
Sinful from the time my mother conceived me.

Surely you desire truth in the inner parts;
You teach me wisdom in the inmost place
.Cleanse me with hyssop, and I will be clean;
Wash me, and I will be whiter than snow.

Let me hear it joy and gladness;
That the bones you have crushed rejoice.
Hide your face from my sins
And block out all my iniquity.

Create in me a pure heart, O God
And renew a steadfast spirit within me.
Do not cast me from your presence
Or take your Holy Spirit from me.
Restore to me the joy of your salvation
And grant me a willing spirit, to sustain me.

(Ps.51:1-12)

David the king of Israel deliberately chose to become involved in a relationship with Bathsheba, another man's wife. To cover up his sin he arranged to have Uriah her husband lose his life in battle by placing him in the most dangerous area of conflict and then having the troops retreat to a safe place leaving the man to face certain death. When this was accomplished, David married Bathsheba after a 'respectful' period of time and carried on with life as if nothing had happened. However the wheels of God's judgment and justice move forward even if at times we perceive them to be moving slowly. Eventually David is confronted by the prophet Nathan. He readily admits his sin, acknowledges his guilt and pleads for the mercy and forgiveness of God. Psalm 51 is that prayer of confession.

Perhaps we have not acted in such a manner as David who coveted, stole, committed adultery and murder, but we have our own sins that need to be confronted. We have fallen short of our own ideals as well as God's standards. But God is a forgiving God.

When the apostles began to preach they proclaimed the Lord's forgiveness to those who repented and believed. Peter preaching to the crowd that had gathered at Solomon's Colonnade declared "Repent, then and turn to God, so that your sins might be wiped out…" (Acts.3:19). Forgiveness of our sins is possible because Christ 'bore our sins' on the cross. When we come to Christ and acknowledge we are sinners and need God's grace and mercy, we are released from the penalty of sin by faith in Jesus Christ. Since Christ paid the debt for our sins we are no longer under judgment and condemnation. The apostle Paul writes: "Therefore there is now no condemnation for those who are in Christ Jesus, because through Jesus Christ the law of the Spirit of life has set me free from the law of sin and death" (Romans 8:1-2).

If we desire to be forgiven of our sins there is the necessity of confessing our sins. John wrote "If we say that we have no sin we deceive ourselves, and the truth is not in us: but, if we confess our sins, He is faithful and just to forgive our sins, and to cleanse us from all unrighteousness' (1John 1:8-9). This indicates very clearly that the forgiveness of our sins by God is conditional upon our confession of our sins. That is why we cannot take sin lightly nor deny what we have done. We need to be honest and transparent before God if we desire our relationship with him to be restored.

Finding forgiveness is just the beginning of the journey. The rest of our life is a process whereby we seek to live for Christ and become more and more like him. However this new relationship with God is not without its challenges. There will be times when we resist God, there will be times when we struggle with temptations and there will be times when we succumb to them. Most of us can echo the words of the apostle Paul, "I do not understand what I do. For what I want to do I do not do, but what I hate I do. … For what I do is not the good I want to do; no, the evil I do not want to do - I keep on doing." (Romans 7:13, 15)

Because we live with the reality of doing what we don't want to do and not doing what we desire to do, our relationship with God can be adversely affected. As we grow in our relationship with God and have a deeper understanding of Him, we become aware of the distance or the gap between our calling as children of God and our behaviour as his devoted followers. We are aware of our destructive thoughts, attitudes, and behaviour, and we feel uncomfortable in God's presence. In fact we feel guilty.

Many do not understand the nature of guilt. Consequently they will feel guilty when in fact they are not guilty. From a biblical perspective guilt is a state or condition when I violate God's laws. I have sinned and I am guilty. In Psalm 51 David knows he is guilty because he violated God's laws. He coveted, stole, committed adultery, arranged for the death of an innocent man, and therefore declares 'I have done what is evil in your sight" (Psalm 51: 4).

In our culture guilt is often described as a feeling. People say 'I feel guilty', which is a subjective statement. We need to be able to distinguish between true guilt and false guilt. To do this we simply ask the question, 'have I violated God's law'? If the answer is yes, then I need to confess my sin and trust in the atoning sacrifice of Christ for forgiveness. If the answer is no, I need to recognize this is false guilt. Some people have an extremely sensitive conscience and the best way for them to deal with false guilt is to have clear teaching about God's grace and forgiveness. We also need to be aware that guilt feelings may arise from the attacks of the enemy. When Satan attacks us with false guilt, he seeks to destroy us. When we are confronted with true guilt God points us to his mercy and grace in order that our relationship with him might be restored and that we might be built up in our 'holy faith'.

EXERCISES

The following exercise are intended to allow you to experience praying with Scripture over a period of seven days and each day will focus upon a specific type of prayer.

DAY 1. CONFESSION

DAY 1

1. Read Ps. 32.

a. What is the source of happiness?

b. How would you describe the struggle this individual was experiencing?

c. How did God treat this person?

d. What is the outcome of confession?

2. Take some time to reflect on your own life. Are you aware of anything that is a barrier between you and God? Write this out in your journal.

3. *Offer this confession as a prayer to God. When you conclude give thanks to God for His mercy and kindness toward you.*

4. *Don't dwell on the past; it is behind you, therefore move forward in God's grace.*

5. *The following prayer of confession is one you may choose to use from time to time.*

A PRAYER OF CONFESSION

Most merciful God,
I confess that I have sinned against you
In my thoughts, by my words and by my actions,
By what I have done,
And by what I have left undone.

I have not loved you with my whole heart;
I have not loved my neighbour as myself.
I am truly sorry and I humbly repent.

For the sake of your Son Jesus Christ,
Have mercy on me and forgive me,
So that I may delight in your will,
And Walk in your ways,
To the glory of your Name.

Amen

(Adapted from the Book of Common Prayer)

REPENTANCE

Repentance and confession are closely linked, but I would suggest that confession precedes repentance. The word repentance literally means 'a change of mind'. In order for this to occur one must first declare or confess what they have done wrong in order to make the necessary and appropriate changes. Some suggest that repentance validates one's confession because if we do not have a change in life the confession is little more than words.

In the Scriptures we see confession followed by acts of repentance. When Paul was preaching in the city at Ephesus many people came to believe in the Lord Jesus Christ and they openly confessed some of the evil practices in which they engaged. A number of these people practiced sorcery and when convicted by the Holy Spirit that this was wrong, they brought their scrolls and burned them publicly. We are told the value of the scrolls was 50,000 drachmas, a drachma being the equivalent of a day's wage. It was through this public act of repentance the word of the Lord spread widely. (Acts 19:18-20)

The act of repentance is most effective when we have an inner desire to change our life so we can become more like Christ. The ability to change comes through empowerment by the Holy Spirit as we yield our lives unto him.

GUIDELINES FOR REPENTANCE:

Douglas Rumford suggests the following three steps in an act of repentance.[3]

Choose to renounce the sinful behaviour.

One who repents makes an intentional break with habits behaviours and actions. This can be done with a simple yet extremely powerful prayer in which one says, "in the name of Jesus Christ, I confess and renounce the sin of [fill in the specific sin]. I declare that I no longer desire to participate in this thought, word, or deed. I rely upon the grace and indwelling power of the Holy Spirit to set me free and who enables me to be conformed to the image of Jesus Christ."

Choose a new behaviour that honours God, others, and yourself.

Recall the parable of Jesus that warned against halfway repentance. He told of the spirit that was cast out returning to the 'house' (i.e. the person) he had left and finding the house clean and swept and put in order, but nothing had been done to fill the house with the protection and power to resist the evil spirit – so it returned with seven other spirits. "And the final condition of that man is worse than the first" (Luke11:26). It isn't enough to part with sin – we must embrace God to be safe!

Make yourself accountable.

We need to rely on other people for support and accountability. We may choose one person or a small group to whom we can entrust ourselves, being confident that the one(s) we have chosen loves and cares about us, and desires our spiritual growth and development. Regardless of who we choose we need to realize we cannot 'go it alone'.

EXERCISE:

DAY 2 REPENTANCE

DAY

2

1. Consider the following questions asked by the accountability groups under the leadership of John Wesley. How would you respond to these questions?

   a) What known sins have you committed since our last meeting?

   b) What temptations have you met with?

   c) How were you delivered?

   d) What have you said, thought, or done, of which you doubt whether it be sin or not.

   e) Have you nothing you desire to keep secret? [4]

2. Take some time to review your life. Ask God to reveal any sinful area in your life that needs to change. Write it down in your journal.

3. What steps will you take to make this happen? Be specific.

4. Will you hold yourself accountable to anyone so that you will have someone to talk to, to pray with and to ask you the hard questions?

5. Read slowly the prayer by St. Francis...

REJOICING AT REPENTANCE
Merciful father,
You rejoice more over one sinner who repents
than over ninety nine righteous souls
who do not need to repent.
And so it is with great joy
now we hear the story
of the shepherd of happiness
as he brings back on his shoulders
the sheep that went astray,
and the of the coin returned
to the treasury
while the neighbours celebrate with the woman
who found it;
and the rejoicing in your house
brings tears of joy
when the story is read
of the younger son
who died and came back to life,
who was lost and found again.
You rejoice in us and in your angels
made holy through your holy love;
you indeed are always the same
never changing in your manner of being;
you know all those things
that do not last forever and
that are not unchanging [5]

EXAMINATION OF CONSCIENCE

Self examination and confession of sin go together since this process helps to clarify our vision and understanding of who we are before God and one another. Confession is necessary because our sins separate us from God. Isaiah declared "Your iniquities have made a separation between you and your God, and your sins have hid his face from you so that he does not hear" (Isaiah 59:2). However sin does not need to separate us from God. John declared "If we confess our sins, he is faithful and just and will forgive our sins and cleanse us from all unrighteousness" (I John.1:9). A deliberate expression of this discipline is called 'examination of conscience' or 'prayer of examen'.

The Psalmist declares, "Lord, you examine me and know me." (Psalm 139:1). David states, "The Lord searches the mind and understands every plan and thought" (1Chronicles 28:9).

And the apostle Paul reminds us that "the Spirit searches all things, even the deep things of God" (1Corinthians 2:10). Since God knows us intimately and thoroughly, it is essential that we do not shrink from self knowledge. As we are open and honest with ourselves we are able to see who we are and seek to make appropriate changes that, by the help of the Holy Spirit we will become all God desires us to be.

The prayer of Examen is a method of examining or reflecting upon ones life in such a manner you do not allow your days to go by unnoticed and in the process you discover how to love and serve God more fully. This prayer covers a very limited period of time, most often it is a recollection and reflection on the events of the past twenty four hours.

Developed years ago by St. Ignatius, this has become a form of prayer to help people enter into the presence of God in a more experiential manner and discover the different ways he reveals himself in our daily life. St. Ignatius encouraged people to become aware of and explore their deepest feelings and desires. Those feelings that help connect us with God he referred to as 'consolations' and those feelings that disconnect us with God he referred to as 'desolations'. As I reflect upon my day, am I aware of having drawn closer to God or am I aware of having moved away from God. Ignatius believed God would speak through these feelings and desires, but first I must become aware of what I am experiencing and seek to understand what is happening.

The Prayer of Examen is very flexible and simple to use as part of a daily routine. Some people set aside two brief periods a day to pray this prayer, but most find it helpful to set aside ten minutes before going to bed to reflect on their day.

As you begin this prayer it is important to take time to become quiet. Find a place where you will not be disturbed, sit comfortably and become relaxed. Remember, you are about to enter into deep and intimate conversation with Jesus.

There are five steps to the Prayer of Examen which can easily be followed, and once you have established a routine of praying in this manner you will learn the approach that fits you best.

BASIC STEPS:

STEP ONE: RECALL THE PRESENCE OF GOD
"In God we live and have our being" Acts.17:28

Every day is filled with a variety of events and experiences. Some days are relaxed while others are filled with tension. Some days are productive while others are challenging. In the centre of all this God is present. So it is important to learn to slow down and reflect upon God's presence. We understand theologically he is always present, but in prayer we place ourselves in his presence in an attentive manner. God the Father loves and cares for you in the deepest possible way. Through Jesus Christ you know of your significance and value to God and the Holy Spirit leads you into all truth so that you may know God more fully. So in this prayer begin by asking God to reveal himself to you.

STEP TWO: ASK THE HOLY SPIRIT TO HELP YOU
"When the Spirit of Truth comes He will guide you into all truth" John.16:13

Ask the Holy Spirit to give you sensitivity as you look over your day, to be able to see the various ways God has been working in your life. The Spirit gives you freedom to look at your life in a way that is neither destructive nor condemnatory. Some feel this is a time to be really hard on yourself. In fact it is an opportunity to see the ways you have responded to the gifts God has given to you in the day. Ask that you will learn and grow as you reflect on these issues and in this manner you will deepen your knowledge of yourself and your relationship with God.

STEP THREE: LOOK OVER YOUR DAY WITH GRATITUDE
"Give thanks to the Lord for He is good, His love endures forever." Psalm. 136:1

Begin by giving thanks to God for all that He has given to you in the day. Some will start from the moment they woke up and recall the events of the day. What happened during your day? What are the events that come to mind? The purpose of this is not to become critical of yourself but rather to be an observer of your life. The following questions might help you in this part of the prayer.

* Was it a good day or a bad day?
* Did anything special happen in this day? A beautiful sunset that captured a memory? A song that stirred you? A critical comment that wounded your spirit?
* Who are some of the people you encountered? What was that experience like?
* How did you feel about these experiences?

A key factor in this step is to become aware of your feelings as you process the day. If there is a deep sense of peace and consolation you feel closer to God. However if you are feeling distressed and upset you need to explore the source of these feelings and how it has moved you away from God. Taking all of this into consideration you need to see how you are moved to express gratitude to God.

STEP FOUR: REVIEW YOUR DAY

"Test yourselves to see whether you are living in faith; examine yourselves. Perhaps you do not realize that Jesus Christ is in you." 2 Corinthians 13:5

This is the longest part of the prayer exercise. Recall the events of the day to see the way you reacted. You may find that at times your heart is divided, wavering between helping and neglecting, listening and ignoring, criticizing and encouraging. This is not meant to be a time to dwell on your failures but rather a time to see how you responded to God's gifts and opportunities. It is a time to see how actively you sought the presence of God in all you were doing and what difference this made.

Where did you love? Did you act freely towards others in a manner that was without an ulterior motive and you simply wanted to 'be there' for them?

Are there habits you've gotten into that just seem to jump into place whenever you are in a typical situation? Do these help or hinder relationships?

Where have I failed?

These simple questions help you become more focused on bringing Christ into every situation and circumstance of your life. You may find things you desire to change but do not seem to have the willpower to do so. This is what you offer to God so that by the power of the Holy Spirit you will be changed into the person God desires you to be.

STEP FIVE: RECONCILE AND RESOLVE
"As the clay is in the potter's hand so you are in mine" Jeremiah 18:6

The final step in the Prayer of Examen is an honest, open, transparent talk, with the Lord. In the initial two steps, you looked at your day with gratitude. In the third and fourth steps you asked God to guide you as you reviewed your actions. At this step you may be led to ask God for forgiveness, for direction, or simply to express gratitude for all He has done. So give thanks that God enabled you to move forward in your relationship with him. If there are areas of life that need to be confessed remember his desire is to allow you to experience healing grace and forgiveness. Be resolved to move forward in a different manner as you acknowledge you are a recipient of God's grace and mercy. Paul expressed it in these words "If anyone is in Christ, you are a new creation; the old has gone the new has come" (1 Corinthians 5:17)

EXERCISE:

To become familiar with this concept of prayer, practice the Prayer of Examen each evening. Use the following statement to help voice your prayer.

Today I am grateful for:
a.

b.

c.

d.

e.

Today I saw God in my life when ...

I felt disconnected to God when ...

I need to accept that ...

Tomorrow I want to do ...

My prayer to God is ...

Try this form of prayer for one week. At the end of the week, if you have found this exercise to be helpful you might consider doing this prayer exercise for a month.

GUIDELINES:

1. Set aside ten minutes each day for this prayer. Choose a time that will work for you but avoid those times when you feel sleepy or tired.

2. Choose a location that is quiet and where you will not be disturbed.

3. Sit comfortably in a chair with your feet on the floor. Sit quietly for a couple of minutes. Take some deep breaths to allow the stress or fatigue to be released.

4. Now begin to recall your day as you slowly reflect upon the theme or question. Ignatius of Loyola focused upon two themes. The first was consolation(that which drew him closer to God) and the second was desolation (that which moved him away from God)

5. You are encouraged to write out this prayer in your daily prayer journal.

For the remaining days in this week you may wish to use the Prayer of Examen and focus upon a fruit of the spirit as a theme to help you draw closer to God.

DAY 3: LOVE

DAY 4: JOY

DAY 5: PEACE

WEEK FOUR

DAY 6: PATIENCE

DAY 7: KINDNESS

Endnotes:

1. John Stott, *Confess Your Sins* ((London; Hodder and Stoughton Limited) 1964 pg 1.

2. Maxie Dunnam, *The Workbook on the Spiritual Disciplines* (Nashville: The Upper Room) 1984 pg. 65

3. Douglas Rumford, *Soul Shaping* (Wheaton: Tyndale Press) 1996 pg. 145

4. Michael Henderson, *John Wesley's Class Meetings: A Model for Making Disciples* (Evangel Publishing House) 1997 pg 118-119

5. Paula Clifford, *Praying with St. Augustine* (London: Triangle Press) 1984 pg.92

PRAYER OF LAMENT

Our lives are not always **filled** with **joy,** happiness and strength.

We know brokenness and pain, alienation and confusion, doubt and the absence of God. When we feel God has abandoned us we easily identify with the words of Jesus as he was dying on the cross "my God, my God, why have you forsaken me?" (Ps.22:2). This is the Prayer of Lament!

Lament is a response to the pain and struggle we experience in life, and one of the places we discover the language of lament is in the psalms. Allender states: "many songs reflect the struggle of the people of God to comprehend the vicissitudes of their lives in the light of God's promise to protect and sustain. What were they to do with God's promises when their forces were devastated in a battle? How are they to trust God when he promised "if you make the Most High your dwelling, even the Lord, who is my refuge, then no harm will befall you, no disaster will come near your tent" (Psalm 91:9-10)? The data of life then and now seems to invite us to doubt rather than to rest in confidence. The psalms tackled this discrepancy of promise and lived reality with forthrightness and the depth of emotion." [1]

At times the lament was a cry of agony as the person struggled to figure out why things happened in such a painful manner and why God ever allowed it to happen.

"O Lord God Almighty, how long will your anger smoulder against the prayers of your people? You have fed them with the brand of tears; you have made them drink tears by the bowlful. You have made us a source of contention to our neighbours, and our enemies mock us." (Psalm 80:4-6).

As the psalmist cries out to God in pain, we discover behind the pain there is a great deal of anger. This aspect of lament is often overlooked in our culture since many have learned to mask their emotions and in some instances any expression of anger is not permitted. We simply accept our lot in life and inwardly seethe with rage. Such an approach was foreign to biblical writers. The psalmist declared:

"You gave us up to be devoured like sheep and have scattered us among the nations. You sold your people for a pittance, gaining nothing from their sale. You have made us a reproach to our neighbours, the scorn and derision of those around us.

All this happened to us, though we had not forgotten you or been false to your covenant.

Our hearts had not turned back; our feet had not strayed from your path. But you crushed us and made us a haunt for jackals and covered us with deep darkness. If we had forgotten the name of our God or spread at our hands to a foreign god, would not God have discovered it, since he knows the secrets of the heart?
Yet for your sake we faced death all day long; we are considered as sheep to be slaughtered.

Awake O Lord! Why do you sleep? Rouse yourself! Do not reject us forever.
Why do you hide your face and forget our misery and oppression?
We are brought down to the dust; our bodies cling to the ground.
Rise up and help us; redeem us because of your unfailing love."
(Psalm 44:11-13; 17-26).

The cry of lament also reveals confusion. Sometimes the writer is searching for answers that are not forthcoming.

"I cried out to God for help; I cried out to God to hear me. When I was in distress, I sought the Lord; at night I stretched out untiring hands and my soul refused to be comforted.
I remembered you, O God, and I groaned; I mused, and my spirit grew faint. You kept my eyes from closing; I was too troubled to speak.
I thought about the former days, the years of long ago; I remembered my songs in the night. My heart mused and my spirit inquired:

"Will the Lord reject forever? Will he never show his favour again? Has his unfailing love vanished forever? As his promise failed for all time? As God forgotten to be merciful? Has he in anger withheld his compassion?" (Psalm 77:1-9).

Many Christians are uncomfortable with these raw emotions and believe it is wrong to express them in such a manner. To deny or suppress these feelings is not healthy, because our feelings are real and they won't go away. Lament is a constructive way to deal with these emotions as we give them to God. Westermann states: "the function of lament is to provide a structure for crisis, hurt, grief, or despair; to move the worshipper from hurt to joy, from darkness to light, from desperation to hope." [2]

In the church, the use of the psalms of lament has been minimal simply because we are not used to embracing the negative aspects of life. Brueggemann suggests the psalms of lament are really a bold act of faith because "it insists that the world must be experienced as it really is and not in some pretended way ... It is bold because it insists that all such experiences of disorder are a proper subject for discourse with God. There is nothing out of bounds, nothing precluded or inappropriate. Everything property belongs in this conversation of the heart. To withhold part of life from that conversation is in fact to withhold part of life from the sovereignty of God". [3]

He then concludes. "these psalms lead us into dangerous acknowledgment of how life really is. They lead us into the presence of God where everything is not polite or simple". [4]

The prayers of lament may be either personal or corporate. Realizing the Psalter is the hymn-book of the people of God, there are two implications. First it is intended to be expressed in a corporate setting, and second it is set to music. To fail to recognize these factors loses the thrust of the psalms. Again this is troublesome for many people. Our corporate worship tends to be celebratory. Even if we are in the midst of pain and turmoil we try to ignore what is going on and at least pretend to be happy as we worship together.

In addition the songs of lament are sung in a minor key which is hardly celebratory and when we gather for corporate worship most people do not want to enter into the pain of others. Michael Card states: "Our failure to lament cuts us off from each other. If you and I are to know one another in a deep way, we must not only share our hurts, anger and disappointment with each other(which we often do), we must also lament them together before the God who hears and is moved by out tears. ... The degree to which I am willing to enter into the suffering of another person reveals the level of my commitment and love for them. If I am not interested in your hurts, I am not really interested in you". [5]

As we examine the psalms of lament, the full range of emotions is experienced and expressed. Every psalm of lament, except Psalm 88, ends on a note of praise. From the viewpoint of prayer the meaning is very clear: once we lament, healing can begin. In order to pray these psalms, and to articulate our own lament it is helpful to understand the basic simple structure of these prayers. Brueggemann has developed an outline whereby the lament is divided into two main sections: plea and praise. [6]

PLEA

* The writer begins with a complaint that reveals to God how serious the situation is. It may describe sickness, isolation, imprisonment, but most often it speaks about death
* There is a crying out to God that he show mercy, or bring about justice, because he is able to do so.
* In order to urge God to act, the writer often provides motivation to give God reason to act. Some of these factors are the person is innocent and needs to be vindicated, or if the person is guilty he or she has repented. The final appeal to God is based on the fact that God consider his own power, position or prestige.

PRAISE

This part of the psalm is different in that there is a substantial change. Things are different; the sense of urgency and desperation has changed to joy and gratitude. There is a movement from plea to praise.

* First there is the assurance of being heard.
* Second there is the payment of vows. In a time of trouble the speaker promised he would pay a vow if God rescued him. Now he is keeping his word as an act of faithfulness.
* Finally there is praise. Previously God had been accused, now he is seen as generous and faithful.

This basic structure reminds us there is a process one moves through in the prayers of lament. It also ought to be a reminder that praise does not come quickly.

The following exercises will look at different aspects of lament as people experienced unique challenges in life. Possibly you will identify with some of these.

EXERCISE:

DAY 1. COMMUNAL PSALMS OF LAMENT

The communal psalms of lament were usually precipitated by a crisis. The entire community was called together to pray and to seek the face of God. At times they would engage in rituals such as fasting, abstinence, wearing of sackcloth, and sprinkling their head with ashes and dust as a sign of mourning. All this was part of the observance as the community lamented.

The crisis might be an invading army, or a plague of locusts. Whatever the crisis, the entire community was affected by it and they came together to cry out to God.

Read Psalm 80

This psalm reveals the deep anguish of the people at the sweeping away of the nation of Israel.

a. How would you describe the petition?

b. What is the lament expressed in vs. 4-7?

c. Describe what God has done for these people in the past? Vs.8-11

d. In. vs.12-13, the petitioner asks why? Is this seen as an attack again God?

e. Finally there is a decision to remain faithful to God. Vs.18-19. How does one get to this place?

Think about the community to which you belong. It may be your family, your church, or your country. Write a prayer of communal lament that expresses the concerns you face as a community.

DAY 2. INDIVIDUAL PSALMS OF LAMENT

DAY 2

Individual laments are different from communal laments in that the troubles of the individual are different from that of a community. It is a personal issue. For example, Samuel's mother Hannah desperately wanted to have a child yet she was unable to conceive. Sadness overwhelmed her and life seemed to be unbearable. Every year she went with her husband and the extended family to Shiloh to worship and sacrifice to the Lord, but we are told that Hannah had no joy in her heart.

"In bitterness of soul Hanna wept much and prayed to the Lord. And she made a vow, saying, "O Lord Almighty, if you will only look upon your servant's misery and remember me, and not forget your servant but give her a son, and I will give him to the Lord for all the days of his life and no razor will ever be used upon his head". (1 Samuel 1:10-11)

In this story we see the lament of a person who had a need and expressed her sorrow and pain to God

Read Psalm 13

This psalm tells about a life situation an individual faces and how he raised many questions before he came to the final conclusion.

a. What are the four questions asked?

b. What do these four questions reveal about the individual's life?

c. The lament is followed by a petition. Express this petition in your own words.

d. In verse five there is a notable change in the psalm. What has changed?

e. The psalm ands with praise. How do you account for this?

f. Do you see the pattern of the psalm of lament? Can you state the basic steps in your own words

Reflect upon your own life. If you are going through a period of difficulty write a prayer of lament based on the structure described by Bruggemann.

DAY 3. THE LAMENT OF JOB

There are many other prayers of lament besides those found in the Psalter. The following exercises will give you an opportunity to explore some of these prayers and discover how people in their distress presented their concerns to God.

When we think of people who experienced great suffering we immediately turn to Job. This man had everything and he lost everything. In this process he made a remarkable statement "shall we not accept good from God, and not suffering?" (Job.2:10) Most wonder how it is possible for someone to get to the place in life where they can say "regardless of what happens to me I will choose to trust God".

Read Job 3

a. What elements of complaint do you discover in this passage?

b. Can you hear the anguish in Job's voice? How would you identify it?

c. How close does Job come to cursing God? What statement of Job comes close to impinging God's wisdom, power and goodness?

If you're able read the entire book of Job at one sitting. When you finish reading the book look at the questions God raises in chapters 40-41. How would you answer them?

DAY 4. THE LAMENT OF JEREMIAH (PART 1)

Jeremiah sometimes referred to as the 'weeping prophet' had a difficult assignment from God. At an early age God called him to be a prophet.

"Before I formed you in the womb I knew you, before you were born I set you apart; I appointed you as a prophet to the nations". (Jeremiah 1:5)

Early in his ministry God warned him that life would not be easy.

"Get yourself ready! Stand up and say to them whenever I command you. Do not be terrified by them, or I will terrify you before them. Today I have made you a fortified city, and iron pillar and a bronze wall to stand against the whole land – I gave the Kings of Judah, its officials, it's Princes and the people of the land. They will fight against you but will not overcome you, for I am with you and will rescue you". (Jeremiah 1:17-19)

DAY

3

DAY

4

As Jeremiah begins in his ministry the word of the Lord came true. The people did not respond to his message. His words bounced off deaf ears and hardened hearts. He experienced public shame and humiliation. People insulted him, beat him, threw him down a dry cistern and left him to die.

To say Jeremiah is upset is an understatement. In a forthright manner he tells God how he feels. But it is through his cry of lament that Jeremiah comes to a new understanding of God and his relationship with him.

a. Read Jeremiah 20:7-18. You are encouraged to read this prayer out loud as this will help you to experience the deep emotion Jeremiah felt. Read the prayer several times. Allow yourself to be in Jeremiah's place.

b. What accusations does he bring again God?

c. What tensions are present in this prayer? Do you think Jeremiah has become bitter?

d. Note a shift in the prayer vs.11-13. What is happening here? Why does Jeremiah curse the day of his birth? Vs.14

e. The prayer concludes without any resolution. God does not answer him. Do you think he has any consolation from God?

f. Think about your own calling in the ministry God has given to you. Are you experiencing any frustration, difficulty or challenge? Are things not working out exactly the way you anticipated? Write out your prayer of lament to God.

DAY 5. THE LAMENT OF JEREMIAH (PART 2)

DAY
5

Previously we considered the call of Jeremiah and learned of the frustrations he experienced over a span of 40 years. During his ministry the people abandoned God and refused to listen to his prophetic warnings. Eventually the city of Jerusalem was held under siege, the people inside the city were dying from hunger and disease while those outside the city were slain by the Babylonians.

The author of Lamentations, which Jewish and Christian tradition ascribe to Jeremiah, pours out his grief over the destruction of the city of Jerusalem and the desolation of the people. Jeremiah openly acknowledges what the people have done by walking away from God and that God is just in allowing this devastation to occur. But Jeremiah still has hope that God will show mercy to this wayward nation.

a. *Read Lamentations. Try to discover what the author is attempting to convey from the perspective of one who mourns with the people. You might try the ancient method of 'lectio divina' as a way of reading this text.*

b. *Memorize Lamentations 3:20-21*

c. *The following songs have been inspirational for the people of God throughout past and present generations. As you read (sing) these songs try to discover how they speak into your life today.*

THE STEADFAST LOVE [7]

The steadfast love of the Lord never ceases,
His mercies never come to an end
They are new every morning
New every morning
Great is your faithfulness O Lord
Great is your faithfulness.

GREAT IS THY FAITHFULNESS [8]

Great is thy faithfulness, O God my Father
There is no shadow of turning with thee.
Thou changest not, thy compassions they fail not.
As thou hast been thou for ever wilt be.
Refrain
Great is thy faithfulness! Great is thy faithfulness!
Morning my morning new mercies I see:
All I have needed thy hand hath provided
Great is thy faithfulness, Lord unto me!

Summer and winter, spring time and harvest,
Sun moon and stars in their courses above
Join with all nature in manifold witness
To thy great faithfulness, mercy and love.

Pardon for sin and a peace that endureth
Thy own dear presence to cheer and to guide;
Strength for today and bright hope for tomorrow,
Blessings all mine, with ten thousand beside!

DAY 6

DAY 6. THE LAMENT FOR A SON: DAVID

David regarded by many as a greatest leader in the nation of Israel and declared by Yahweh as 'a man after God's own heart', experienced much grief and pain in his family life. One of his children, Amnon fell in love with and subsequently raped his sister Tamor. When David discovered what had taken place we are told he was furious but he did nothing about it. Absalom, a brother of Tamor, was incensed and in a fit of rage plotted and carried out the murder of Amnon. This led to a rift between David and Absalom and Absalom eventually tried to usurp the throne of his father. Eventually the armies of these two men met and engaged in battle with Absalom losing twenty thousand troops. As he fled the battle, riding on a swift mule, his long locks of hair became entangled in the low boughs of a tree and he was left suspended between heaven and earth. Joash the commander of David's army, when informed of Absalom's plight went to the place where he was hanging and killed him. He carried out this action in spite of the fact David had commanded Absalom's life be spared.

David, waiting for news of the battle, was devastated when he heard about the death of his son. There was no rejoicing for his heart was broken. He cried out; "O my son Absalom! My son, my son Absalom! If only I had died instead of you – O Absalom, my son, my son!" (2 Samuel 18:33)

Those who have issues with their children or have seen strife and bitterness in their family can identify to some degree with David's pain and understand the agony of his lament.

a. Read Psalm 63. This psalm was written by David when he was fleeing from Absalom during the time Absalom was trying to usurp his father's throne.

b. Try to identify with David's struggle with his son. What do you think he is experiencing?

c. Read 2 Samuel 18. At verse thirty three explore the pain of a father whose son has died with the knowledge that the relationship between the father and son had died long before this event. Write down your thoughts.

d. If you have a broken relationship that seems beyond repair write out your prayer of anguish and sadness.

e. If you have lost someone who is close to you read the hymn "Go Silent Friend"

GO SILENT FRIEND [9]

Go silent friend,
Your life has found its ending;
To dust returns
Your weary mortal frame.
God, who before birth
Called you into being,
Now calls you hence,
His accent still the same.

Go silent friend,
Your life in Christ is buried;
For you he lived
And died and rose again.
Close by his side
Your promised place is waiting
Where, fully known,
You shall with God remain.

Go silent friend,
Forgive us if we grieved you;
Safe now in heaven,
Kindly say our name.
Your life has touched us,
That is why we mourn you;
Our lives with that you
Cannot be the same.

Go silent friend,
We do not grudge you glory;
Sing, sing with joy
Deep praises to your Lord.
You who believed
That Christ would come back for you
Now celebrate
That Jesus keeps his word.

DAY
7

DAY 7. THE LAMENT OF JESUS:

The bible tells us that Jesus was acquainted with sorrow and struggle. Isaiah describes his life in this way.

"He grew up before him like a tender shoot, and like a root out a dry ground. He had no beauty or majesty to attract us to him, nothing in his appearance that we should desire him. He was despised and rejected by men, a man of sorrows, and familiar with suffering. Like one from whom many hid their faces he was despised and we esteemed him not. Surely he took up our infirmities and carried our sorrows". (Isaiah 53: 2-4)

During his three years of ministry, Jesus experienced misunderstanding, rejection and even hatred by people. When he came to his own village he could do no great works of their because of their lack of faith. The religious authorities of his day were threatened by him and sought at every occasion not only to undermine his ministry but to have him destroyed.

The culmination of his ministry was at the cross, where Jesus took upon himself the sins of the world. Such an act meant he would receive not only the judgment of God, but also be forsaken by God. To come to this place of surrender was not easy. Jesus went to the Garden of Gethsemane where he agonized all night over the decision until he was able to say 'not my will but yours'.

As his life was expiring Jesus cried out with a great wail of lament the prayer that he had been taught from his childhood "my God, my God, why have you forsaken me?"

a. Read Psalm 22

b. Take some time to reflect upon your life and note any experience of abandonment. Note any verses in Psalm 22 that speak particularly to your situation.

c. Pray today for people who are abandoned. Refugees, runaway children, street people, prisoners, those who suffer from dementia, the elderly, the poor.

d. This day discover how you might offer a simple act of kindness toward someone who feels abandoned.

Endnotes:

1. Dan Allender, The Hidden Hope of Lament www.leaderu.com/marshill.1994 pg.2

2. Claus Westermann, The Psalms: Structure, Content and Message (Minneapolis: Augsburg Publishing House) 1980 pg. 4

3. Walter Brueggemann, The Message of the Psalms (Minneapolis: Augsburg Publishing House) 1984 pg. 52

4. ibid. pg 53

5. Michael Card, A Sacred Sorrow (Colorado Springs: Nav. Press) 2005 pg.29

6. Brueggemann op.cit., pg. 54-57

7. Robert Webber, Vicky Tusken, John Witvleit, Jack Schrader, Renew! Songs and Hymns for Blended Worship (Carol Stream: Hope Publishing House) 1998 pg. 23

8. ibid. pg. 249

9. John L. Bell, Graham Maule, When Grief is Raw (Glasgow: Wild Goose Publications) 1997 pg. 74

PETITIONARY PRAYER

I love the Lord for he heard My voice;

He heard my cry for mercy.

Because he turned his ear to Me,

I will call upon him as long as I live.

(Psalm 116:1-2)

Prayers of petition or intercession are perceived by some as simply bringing a 'shopping list' of requests to God with the hope and expectation he will answer our needs. Because of this some speak disparagingly about petitionary prayer. In contrast Anthony Bloom states,

"People seem to think that petition is the lowest level of prayer; then comes gratitude, then praise. But in fact it is gratitude and praise that are expressions of a lower relationship. On our level of half belief it is easier to sing hymns of praise or thank God than to trust him enough to ask something in faith. Even people who believe half heartedly can turn to thank God when something nice comes their way; and there are moments of elation when everyone can sing to God. But it is much more difficult to have such undivided faith as to ask with one's whole heart and whole mind with complete confidence. No one should look askance at petition, because the ability to say prayers of petition is a test of the reality of our faith." [1]

WEEK SIX

There are times when we find ourselves praying for others; our family, friends, co-workers or those in our faith community. The issues before us are many and varied, from health concerns, to financial issues, to children in trouble, or a crisis of faith. One of the first prayers of intercession noted in the scriptures was that of the patriarch Abraham interceding on behalf of his nephew Lot and his family living in the city of Sodom, the place God was going to destroy. (Genesis 18:16-33)

Moses prayed for the children of Israel throughout his lifetime. Once during their wilderness wanderings the Israelites designed a golden calf they could worship. God's anger at such idolatry was such that he decided to destroy these people. Moses pleaded with God to show mercy and 'the Lord relented and did not bring on his people the disaster he had threatened." (Exodus 32:14)

The early church interceded for Peter while he was in prison and they were quite surprised when his release occurred. (Acts 12) We are told he went to the home of the mother of John Mark and discovered that "many people gathered and were praying" for his release. Would Peter's freedom from prison have occurred without the prayers of this faith community? We don't know for sure, but Luke apparently saw a connection between these two events since he included the record of the petitionary prayers in his account of this miracle.

One of the apostle Paul's petitionary prayer for the church at Philippi was that their " love may abound more and more in knowledge and depth of insight so that you may be able to discern what is best and may be pure and blameless until the day of Christ, filled with the fruit of righteousness that comes through Christ Jesus - to the praise and glory of God." (Philippians 1:9-11)

Probably the greatest intercessor of all was the Lord Jesus Christ. The Gospels record several of Jesus' prayers for others. For example he prayed that Peter would not succumb to the evil one but that he would remain strong in his commitment to the Lord. (Luke 22:32). Jesus prayed for those who crucified him. "Father forgive them for they know not what they are doing" (Luke23:34). And while he was on earth he prayed for his followers. In John we read "I pray also for those who will believe in me through their message, that all of them may be one, Father, just as you are in me and I am in you. May they also be in us so that the world will know that you have sent me." (John 17:20-21).

It is so encouraging for the church to realize this ministry of intercession by the Lord Jesus is still ongoing. Grenz states: "This ministry of intercession did not end at his death. Rather the resurrected Lord has ascended to "the right hand of the Father." There as the believers advocate with the Father (1John 2:1), he intercedes on behalf of his own (Romans 8:34). In fact, intercession is the only aspect of the Lord's ministry that the New Testament depicts as continuing after the close of his earthly sojourn"(Hebrews 7:25). (2)

As we offer our prayers of petition we need to understand some basic elements about this type of prayer. Grenz describes petition as "laying hold of and releasing God's willingness and ability to act in accordance with God's will and purpose on behalf of creation that God loves". [3] Grenz sees that petitionary prayer involves the fact that God is willing to act on behalf of his creation because he love us and because he is all powerful, he is able to meet any situation we find ourselves in. Subsequently we must come to a place of dependence upon God, in fact there are situations where God will not act until we come to that awareness. If we think we can handle life on our own then we will not seek God's help.

Petitionary prayer is not only an expression of our dependence upon God it is also an expression of our faith in God's 'willingness and ability to act'. Throughout the New Testament we see that faith brings results. When Jesus went to his home town and began to teach and preach in the synagogue the people were amazed. However they dismissed him as the 'carpenter's son' and refused to see that the wisdom revealed through his teaching and the miracles he performed were evidence of his deity. As a result "he did not do many miracles there because of their lack of faith". (Matthew 13:58)

On the other hand there are people who pray and believe they are acting in faith, yet do not seem to receive any answers to their requests. How do they continue in faith?

In response to this question Dunnam makes a helpful observation. He states "Faith is not a confidence measured in human terms or by human limits. Faith refuses to quit praying even when there seems to be evidence that we are not being heard. We push our confidence and hope beyond apparent defeat and we continue to pray.

[Jesus] spoke to them in a parable to show that they should keep on praying and never lose heart:' There was once a judge who cared nothing for God or man, and in the same town there was a widow who constantly came before him demanding justice against her opponent. For a long time he refused; but in the end he said to himself, 'True, I care nothing for God or man; but this widow is so great a nuisance that I will see her righted before she wears me out with her persistence.' The Lord said, "You hear what the unjust judge says; and will not God vindicate his chosen, who cry out to him day and night, while he listens patiently to them? I tell you he will vindicate them soon enough. But when the Son of Man comes, will he find faith on earth? (Luke 18:1-8)

Someone has made the very helpful distinction between faith in prayer and prayer in faith. Faith can be a perversion. Certainly faith in prayer may be presumptuous and clamourous, presenting ultimatums to God and demanding his acquiescence. But prayer in faith is different. It may ask and keep on asking. Indeed it may be clamorous. But all that the asking and pleading is, is entire submission to the will of God. Our faith is not in the prayer, but in God. In prayer we may plead passionately for our needs, but our faith is in God; thus we can close our petitions as Jesus did, "Thy will be done".

Prayer in faith acknowledges God's sovereignty and rejoices in it. It is confident that all forces are ultimately under God's reign and power and that all things will work together for good for those who love God." [4]

BASIC PRINCIPLES OF 'INTERCESSORY PRAYER'

a. Tell God.

Some will say 'Who am I to tell God what to do?" We need to realize that our relationship with God is exactly that … a relationship. Therefore we are not telling God what to do,we are sharing with him our needs and concerns. Sharing all aspects of our life is integral to developing a relationship of intimacy with God. Paul wrote:

"The Lord is near; have no anxiety, but in everything make your requests known to God in prayer and petition with thanksgiving. Then the peace of God, which is beyond our utmost understanding will keep guard over your hearts and your thoughts in Christ Jesus". (Philippians 4:6-7, NEB)

We begin to see that petition is not telling God what to do, rather we are making known to him our needs. Some believe God already knows what we need and he will do whatever is best for us, therefore we do not presume to tell God anything. This reasoning fails to take into account the fact that our relationship with God is a dynamic one and telling him what our needs and concerns are, is an important element of that relationship. Matthew tells the story of two blind men who followed Jesus and called out, "have mercy on us Son of David". Obviously Jesus knew about their condition and what was best for them was to be able to see. However they first cried out to the Lord and then he asked them if they believed he could heal them to which they replied in the affirmative. Then Jesus said, "according to your faith will it be done to you". (Matthew 8:27-29)

Over and over the scriptures allow us to see the compassionate heart of Jesus toward people in need. This ought to give us courage to bring our petitions to God because we know he cares about us.

b. Be Persistent

How often do we bring a request before God? Do we keep on praying until we receive an answer in the affirmative or do we pray once and leave the results to God? To be honest this is a question that is not easy to answer and an issue many struggle with. On the one hand, if we continually bring an issue before God is this a lack of faith? On the other hand if we continually pray about an issue does it reveal our true desire?

Jesus told a parable that helps us understand the significance of persistence in prayer.

"Suppose one of you has a friend, and he goes to him at midnight and says, 'friend, lend me three loaves of bread, because a friend of mine on the journey has come to me, and I have nothing to set before him.'

"Then the one inside answers, 'Don't bother me. The door is already locked, and my children are with me in bed. I can't get up and give you anything.'

I tell you though he will not get up and gave him the bread because he is his friend, yet because of the man's boldness he will get up and give him as much as he needs.

"So I say to you: ask and it will be given to you; seek and you will find; knock and the door will be opened to you. For everyone who asks receives; he who seeks finds; and to him who knocks, the door will be opened." Luke 11:5-10

At the conclusion of the parable, Jesus said we are to do three things; ask, seek, knock. The verb tense implies a continuous action. So we can translate the text 'keep on asking, keep on seeking, and keep on knocking'. Jesus encourages persistence, and this persistence got results.

A second parable gives us further insight into Jesus teaching about persistence. The story is referred to as the parable of the persistent widow. Jesus told this parable to teach his disciples that they should "always pray and not give up".

"In a certain town there was a judge who neither feared God nor cared about men. And there was a widow in that town that kept coming to him with the plea, 'grant me justice against my adversary.'

"For some time he refused. But finally he said to himself, 'even though I don't fear God or care about men, yet because this widow keeps bothering me, I will see that she gets justice, so that she won't eventually wear me out with her coming!'"

And the Lord said. "Listen to what the unjust judge says. And will not God bring about justice for his chosen ones, who cry out to him day and night? Will he keep putting them off? I tell you he will see that they get justice, and quickly. However, when the Son of Man comes, will he find faith on the earth?" (Luke 18:1-8)

Reflecting on this parable, Grenz states "a widow who is the victim of some injustice, repeatedly pleaded her case to a judge. Although the judge was not a righteous person, eventually her persistence was rewarded, for he pronounced justice on her behalf. The point of the parable is clear. If sustained pleading can move an unrighteous judge, to grant justice, how much more will God, who is the righteous Judge, hear the unfailing pleas of the oppressed disciples of Jesus and bring justice to their cause at the coming of the Son of Man. Steadfastness in praying for the return of the Lord will eventually be honoured. Justice will be done on behalf of God's people for the day of the Lord will come". [5]

As we persist in our prayers there are several things we discover. First our personal faith grows. At times God does not answer us immediately, so when this occurs we need to be patient and learn to wait and trust God is working in way that at the present time we do not fully comprehend. Second we learn how much we desire and need what we are asking for. Through repeated prayer we begin to discern how serious we are about the requests we make to God. Finally, when we persist in prayer and God grants our request, there is an expression of gratitude for what God has done for us.

In scripture it is evident God encourages us to persist in our prayers because God delights to give good gifts to his children. Grenz states "Knowledge of God's love and of God's willingness to give good gifts challenges the disciples to a bold confident prayer. But this places an important limitation on prayer. The believer can rightly persist only in requesting good things from God. Because God is good, and not evil, God can be expected only to give those gifts that are in accordance with God's holy character." [6]

c. Praying in the Name of Jesus

Over and over the scriptures tell us that when we pray we are to pray in Jesus' name. "Whatever you ask in my name I will do it, that the Father may be glorified in the Son." (John 14:13 RSV)

"If you ask anything in my name, I will do it." (John 14:14 RSV)

"You did not choose me but I chose you and appointed you that you should go and bear fruit and that your fruit should abide; so that whatever you ask the Father in my name , he may give it to you." (John 15:16 RSV)

"In that day you will ask nothing of me. Truly, truly, I say to you, if you ask anything of the Father, he will give it to you in my name. Hitherto you have asked nothing in my name; ask and you will receive, that your joy may be full." (John 16:23-24 RSV)

As we read these words we are struck by the repeated invitation of Jesus to pray in his name. For some praying 'In Jesus Name' has just become a way of concluding their prayers without any thought about what is being said. Consequently the meaning and power of praying in the name of Jesus is lost. In addition we must guard against praying and adding these words as a magic formula, believing that saying the words 'in the name of Jesus' somehow gets God's attention.

In the Bible the names of a person were believed to bear descriptive significance. Dunnam states "as we pray in the name of Jesus we are praying in the powerful love of Jesus, because love was the supreme quality of his whole life. … Jesus lived love, taught love, acted love. He was love. He and the Father are one in love for God is love." [7]

"To you whom I love I say, let us go on loving one another for love comes from God. Every man who truly loves is God's son and has some knowledge of him. But the man who does not love cannot know him at all, for God is love.

To us the greatest demonstration of God's love for us has been his sending his only Son into the world to give us life through him. We see real love, not in the fact that we loved God, but that He loved us and sent his Son to make personal atonement for our sins. If God loved us as much as that, surely we, in our turn should love one another!

It is true that no human being has ever had a direct vision of God. Yet if we love one another God does actually live within us, and his love grows in us toward perfection. And as I wrote above, the guarantee of our living in him and his living in us is the share of his Spirit which he gives us." (I John 4:7-13 Phillips)

When we pray in the name of Jesus we need to continually remind ourselves that the person who is the intercessor seeks to be first and foremost a person in Christ. We are people who 'abide in Christ' or pray 'in his name'. Dunnam states: 'the intercessor seeks always to be a person in Christ…We can tap the spiritual power offered by Jesus only to the capacity which we develop by living and acting in the name of Jesus…Everything depends upon our relationship to Christ. The power he has in our life he will express through our prayers. Prayer then emanates through our life not our lips…when Christ has everything of me he will obtain everything for me. If I let him have everything I have, he will give me everything he has." [8] (James 1:19).

DAY 1

EXERCISE:

This week we will focus on Intercessory Prayer. The guidelines are designed to help us pray effectively for ourselves as well as others. Seven different themes (one for each day) are addressed in this prayer exercise.

DAY 1. PRAYING FOR THE FORGIVENESS OF SIN

In the Lord's Prayer we pray "Forgive us our sins as we forgive those who sin against us." (Matthew 6:12) This petition has a qualification attached to it. We can only ask God to forgive us to the extent we forgive others.

We forgive because we have been forgiven and because we want to follow the example of Jesus. Paul writes "Be kind to one another, tender hearted, forgiving each other, just as God in Christ also has forgiven you." (Ephesians 4:32)

Without forgiveness there are barriers that exist and this leads to bitterness, pain and resentment toward one another.

1. Read Psalm 19:7-18

2. Take some time to think about your relationships. Are you aware of any conflict you have with another? Are there people you hold a grudge against? Describe these issues and offer them to God. Make a decision to forgive those who have hurt you and be released from any bitterness within you.

3. As you are able, seek to express this forgiveness and where possible be reconciled.

4. Make the following prayer your own.

Almighty and everlasting God, who is always more ready to hear than we to pray, and willing to give more than either we desire or deserve: pour down upon us the abundance of your mercy; forgiving us those things where of our conscience is afraid, and giving us those things which we are not worthy to ask, but through the merits and mediation of Jesus Christ, your Son our Lord. Amen (adapted BCP)

Lord Christ, who by your cross and passion reconciled the world to God and broke down the barriers of race and colour which divide people and nations:
Make us all your people
Instruments of reconciliation in the life of our world,
That we may inherit the blessings
Which you promised to the peacemakers. Amen (BBC)

"God was reconciling the world to himself in Christ, not counting our sins against us. And he has committed to us the message of reconciliation....God made him who had no sin to be sin for us, so that in him we might become the righteousness of God." (2 Corinthians 5:19,21)

DAY 2: PRAYING FOR UNITY IN THE BODY OF CHRIST

In John 17 Jesus constantly prays for the unity of the church. He states: "that all of them may be one, Father just as you are in me and I am in you. May they also be in us so that the world may believe that you have sent me". (John 17:21)

Too often the Christian church has divided and split over non essentials. There are many Christians who will have nothing to do with other believers simply because they belong to another denomination. How this must grieve the heart of God! In fact our diviseness may cause some people to reject the gospel of Christ. Jesus prayed that as the world saw unity amongst his followers they would realize this is truly the work of God, for only God can bring together people who are self centred, divisive and critical, into one caring and supportive family.

1. Read Ephesians 4:1-6.

2. Memorize Ephesians 4:3

3. Write or call someone who attends a different church or denomination. Tell them you are praying for them today. Find some way to bring encouragement to them.

4. Include other congregations in your daily prayer. Especially pray for the pastors and leaders that they will be affirmed in their ministry and leadership.

DAY

2

5. *Pray this prayer as part of your daily devotion*

We pray Lord God for your Church throughout the world:
That it may share to the full in the work of your Son,
Revealing you to people
And reconciling people to you;
That Christians may learn to love one another.
As you have loved us;
That your Church may more and more exhibit the unity
Which is your will and your gift.

We pray that we and all Christians
May be what you want us to be,
And do what you want us to do:
That we may be content with whatever comes our way,
And attain peace of mind in self-forgetfulness.

We pray for those who suffer for faith and conviction,
And are tempted to turn back
Because their way is hard:
Help and strengthen them, Lord,
So that they may hold out to the end,
And by their loyal witness draw others to you.

We pray that the Gospel of our Lord Jesus Christ may be
Known and accepted by increasing numbers of people.
Draw to yourself all seekers after truth and goodness:
May they find the unfathomable riches
Which can be found in you alone.
And may all the nations you have made
Come and worship you
And honour your name. [9]

DAY 3. PRAYING FOR SPIRITUAL AWARENESS

DAY

3

The prayer for spiritual awareness is one whereby we receive a new understanding and appreciation of all we are and can become in Christ. Paul prayed this for the Christians in Ephesus.

"I pray also that the eyes of your heart may be enlightened in order that you may know the hope to which he has called you, the riches of his glorious inheritance in the saints." (Ephesians 1:18)

In essence this prayer is a request for an opening of one's spiritual awareness through the working of the Holy Spirit. This includes realizing who and what we are in Christ, becoming aware of the power of God available to us, being aware of the presence of Christ in our lives and experiencing the truth of his promises.

It is easy for Christians to forget some of these amazing truths and we need to continually go back to the scriptures to see what God will do in the lives of those who love and obey him. Sadly, many Christians never experience this spiritual awareness and their lives are less than fulfilled.

1. Read Ephesians 1:15-23

2. What are the specific ways God will 'enlighten' you? What are the promises he makes to you?

3. Choose one aspect that speaks into your life today and make it your prayer. Ask God to allow this to become a reality. What difference will this make in your life?

4. How can you use this prayer as a way to pray for others? Pray this for those whom God places on your heart.

5. Use the following prayer as a means to pray for awareness of God's gifts to you.

*"Lord, all your treasures of wisdom and knowledge are hidden in Christ.
You reveal them through words spoken in his name.*

*Help us to understand what has been done for our redemption,
So that Christ may live in our hearts by faith
And be proclaimed in our lives by love.*

*Give us O Lord, a clear vision of the truth,
Faith in your power, and confident assurance of your presence. Amen"*

DAY 4

DAY 4. PRAYING FOR PROTECTION:

One of the great prayers of protection in the Old Testament is offered by Laban the father in law of Jacob, when Jacob and his family returned home where he would be confronted by his brother Esau. As they departed Laban prayed 'May the Lord watch between me and you while we are absent one from the other' (Genesis 31:49) This prayer is referred to as the 'Mizpah'.

Psalm 91 is another example of a prayer for protection. Quite often this Psalm is recited before sleeping at night.

> He who dwells in the shelter of the Most High will rest
> in the shadow of the Almighty.
> I will say of the Lord, "he is my refuge and my fortress,
> my God in whom I trust." (Psalm 91:1-2)

There is another type of protection we need to consider, that is, protection from the 'evil one'. Jesus in his 'High Priestly' prayer, prayed that the Father would 'protect us from the evil one' (John 17: 15). Peter tells us the devil 'walks about like a roaring lion seeking whom he may devour". (1Peter 5: 8)

Every day we face challenges that can upset us and cause us to be anxious and even afraid. In the midst of it all, the Lord promises to be with us and protect us. Therefore prayers of protection enable us to give our concerns to God and to live with the confidence that he is watching over us.

EXERCISE:

1. Memorize the 'Mizpah'.

2. Read Psalm 91 before going to bed. Let these words be the last thing you think about as you drift into sleep.

3. Be aware that everyday the people of God are in a spiritual struggle. Sometimes it is subtle and other times it is overt. Read Ephesians 6:10-18. As you begin your day mentally put on the various pieces of spiritual armour to protect yourself from the attacks of the enemy.

Note the pieces of armour:
a. belt of truth
b. breastplate of righteousness
c. shoes ... the gospel of peace
d. shield of faith
e. helmet of salvation

4. Throughout the day reflect on the presence of God and his care over you.

DAY 5. PRAYING FOR HEALING

The mission of Jesus can be summarized simply in the words Jesus spoke after his encounter with Zacchaeus 'The son of man has come to seek and to save that which was lost." The word 'salvation' literally means healing or wholeness. Jesus came to bring healing or wholeness to every aspect of our life ... spiritually, emotionally, relationally and physically.

Prayer for healing is something Christians do. At times we are confused or uncertain what God is doing, but we still pray in accordance with the scriptures.

James tells us: "Is anyone among you sick? Then you must call for the elders of the church and they are to pray over you anointing you with oil in he name of the Lord; and the prayer offered in faith will restore the one who is sick , and the Lord will raise that one up , and if sins have been committed they will be forgiven . Therefore confess your sins to one another and pray for one another so that you may be healed. The prayer of a righteous person can accomplish much." (James 5:14-16)

We need to recognize there is a mystery to God's healing ways as we pray for ourselves and for one another. Sometimes the Lord heals people immediately as is evident in many of the healings Jesus performed. However sometimes it is progressive. On one occasion Jesus laid his hands on a blind man, when asked if he could see the man said that he saw people as 'trees walking'. In other words his vision was still blurred. Jesus touched him again and his sight was fully restored.

Paul often healed people. When he was shipped wrecked on the Island of Malta he was bitten by a viper, yet suffered no ill effects. Later the Governor of the Island asked him to see his father who was ill suffering from dysentery and a fever. We are told Paul "went in to see him and after he prayed, he laid his hands upon him and healed him." (Acts 28:8)

On the other hand Paul was unable to heal his friend Trophimus and left him ill at Miletus. (2 Timothy 4:20) Paul also asked the Lord to remove what he termed a 'thorn in the flesh'.

The Lord told him flat out this request would not be granted but Paul would experience something more. The Lord said to him "my grace is sufficient for you, my strength is made perfect in weakness." (2Corinthians 12:9) Knowing this Paul gladly accepted his lot in life.

In our prayer for healing we need to realize God may not respond in the manner we desire. Most have an inner desire to be healed and trust God will grant the request. There are times when God will say yes, times when God will say no, and times when God will say not yet. So we bow before the mystery of God and trust in his sovereign plan.

EXERCISE:

1. Read Luke 6:12-13; 9:1-2

2. Pray the following Litany of Healing

"Let us name before God those for whom we offer our prayers…

God the Father, your will for all people is health and salvation;
We praise and thank you O Lord.

God the Son, you came that we might have life, and have it more abundantly,
We praise and thank you O Lord

God the Holy Spirit, you make our bodies the temple of your presence;
We praise and thank you O Lord.

Holy Trinity, one God, in you we live and move and have our being;
We praise and thank you O Lord.

Lord, grant your healing grace to all who are sick, injured, or disabled, that they may be made whole.
Hear us O Lord of Life

Grant to all who seek your guidance, and to all who are lonely, anxious, or despondent, a knowledge of your will and an awareness of your presence;
Hear us O Lord of Life.

Mend broken relationships, and restore those in emotional distress to soundness of mind and serenity of spirit;
Hear us O Lord of Life.

Grant to the dying peace and a holy death, and uphold by the grace
and consolation of your Holy Spirit those who are bereaved;
Hear us O Lord of life

You are the Lord who does wonders
You have declared your power among the people

With you, O Lord is the well of life:
And in your light we see light.

Hear us O Lord of Life:
Heal us, and make us whole.

Amen." (10)

3. *The following scripture passages are suggested for various circumstances in life.*
   Read the passages slowly and allow God to speak to you.

a. Suffering:

Ps. 88; Matthew 11:28-30; Romans 5:1-5; Romans 8:35-39.

b. God's Presence:

Ps.46:1-7, 10-11; Isaiah 43:1-3a; Isaiah 61:1-3

c. Forgiveness:

Psalm 51:1-2, 7-12; Matthew 9:2-8; 2 Corinthians 5:16-21

d. Patience and Trust:

Psalm 27:1, 4-9, 13-14; Mark 14:36; 1 Peter 4:12-13

e. When Dying

Psalm 23; John 14:1-6; Revelation 21:1-7

4. Prayers for various occasions.

Serenity:

God grant to us
The serenity to accept the things we cannot change,
The courage to change the things we can,
And the wisdom to know the difference;
Through Jesus Christ our saviour.

(Traditional. Ascribed to Reinhold Nebur)

Prayer for Support:

O Lord,
Support us all the day long,
Until the shadows lengthen, the evening comes,
The busy world is hushed,
The fever of life is over,
And our work is done.

Then, Lord in your mercy grant us a safe lodging,
A holy rest,
And peace at last;
Through Jesus Christ our Lord.
Amen.

(John Henry Neuman 19th century)

DAY 6. PRAYING FOR THE NEEDY

DAY 6

In North American we live in an environment where the economy is strong and it seems the rich are getting richer and the poor are getting poorer. The prophet Amos was called to speak to the people of his day during a time of great affluence and peace, to remind them that God is greatly concerned about the poor and the oppressed peoples. Today we would call them the 'marginalized'.

God's call is to justice, righteousness and compassion. As followers of Jesus do we have compassionate hearts? Do we care about the poor? Do we seek justice for the marginalized? How do we pray for them? Does our prayer lead to action?

EXERCISE:

*1. Read the following passages: Amos 1:3-2:3; 2:6-16; Why is God's heart broken?
Do you see a parallel today?*

2. Read Deuteronomy 24:17-18. What are the three lists of people?

3. Who are these people today? Who speaks for them?

4. Read Amos 5: 21-23. What does God really despise?

5. Read Amos 7:1-9. What are the three images of coming judgment?

6. How does your life measure against the plumb line of :

a. Generosity?
b. Serving?
c. Reaching out?

*7. Today pray about specific areas of concern for the marginalized. Read the newspaper to
see some of the obvious needs of people. Volunteer to serve in an inner city mission or food
bank. Give generously to the mission ministry of your church. As you give financially, pray
about the use of this resource. See if there is an opportunity for you to be involved in a mission project in the two thirds world. This will expand your global awareness of the mission
of the church.*

DAY 7. PRAYING FOR YOUR COMMUNITY.

When Joshua was given the leadership of the nation of Israel, the Lord told him "Moses my servant is dead. Now then, you and all these people, get ready to cross the Jordan River into the
land I am about to give to them-to the Israelites, I will give you every place where you set your
foot, as I promised Moses". (Joshua 1:2-3) As they moved forward they claimed the promises
of God and eventually entered the Promised Land.

Over the centuries Christians have utilized 'prayer walks' as a way of praying for their communities and claiming this territory for God.

DAY

7

WEEK SIX

As we develop the habit of prayer walking we see our neighbourhoods in a different manner. We see through the eyes of Christ and become more aware of the spiritual climate in our community and places where there are spiritual strongholds. This helps us in planning ministry strategies. In addition we become more sensitive to those who are living in our communities. We pass places of business, seats of government, halls of learning, centres for recreation and homes where people live. All of this can be a focal point for our prayers.

Another aspect of a prayer walk is simply time to be alone with God and to enjoy his presence and his creation. At times we become so busy and preoccupied we fail to notice all that is around us. As we take time to slow down and enjoy creation our hearts are filled with wonder, joy and gratitude.

David Stone has suggested that the goals of prayer walking are very simple. [11]

a. For Vision: As we walk and pray we begin to see our neighbours through God's eyes.

b. For Relationships: As we pray for our neighbourhoods we make our neighbours aware of the goodness of God.

c. For Hope: Many neighbourhoods are in trouble. Through prayer we bring hope that is found only in God.

EXERCISE:

1. Today plan a prayer walk in your neighbourhood. It might only be the block where you live. Possibly you will extend this walk at a later date.

2. Pray against any evil or spiritual power that might be in opposition to the work of God.

3. Pray for all in leadership at different governmental levels. Pray against any corruption that exists.

4. Pray for a spiritual awakening for the entire area.

Endnotes:

1. http:www.ffoulkes.org/prayer/ch8.php

2. S. Grenz, Prayer The Cry For The Kingdom (Peabody, Mass. Hendrickson Publishing 1988) pg. 15

3. ibid., pg 39

4. M. Dunnam, The Workbook Of Intercessory Prayer (Nashville, Tenn. Upper Room 1979) pg. 24-25

5. Grenz, op.cit. pg. 85

6. ibid., pg. 84

7. Dunnam, op. cit. pg. 91

8. ibid. pg. 128

9. Caryl Micklem, Contemporary Prayers For Public Worship (Grand Rapids, Michigan, Eerdmans 1967) pg. 53

10. Morris Maddocks, A Healing House of Prayer (Toronto Ontario, Hodder and Stoughton 1984) pg. 280

11. http://www.geocities.com/YWAMKerla/Prayerwalk.htm

THANKSGIVING AND PRAISE

Gives thanks to the Lord, for he is good

His love endures forever
Give thanks to the God of gods
His love endures forever.
Give thanks to the Lord of lords:
His love endures forever.
Give thanks to the God of heaven
His love endures forever.
(Ps.136:1-3,26)

Throughout scripture thanksgiving and praise to God is constantly on the lips of his people. When we understand that God is sovereign over all the affairs of life and he is working in and through all our experiences to bring about our ultimate good; we learn to respond by expressing gratitude to him. We recall the assurances of Scripture that we are secure in our relationship with God, surrounded by his love, governed by his perfect justice, and motivated by his enduring promises. We believe God is the very essence of our joy and strength and he is the one who sustains us in all of life. Yet all too often when problems arise we quickly forget these truths, we begin to despair about life and our gratitude vanishes. So is it possible or even realistic to expect people to offer thanksgiving and praise to God regardless of what life brings?

Scripture portrays gratitude as more than a feeling or an emotion we have when everything is going well. Paul, writing to the church in Rome reminds them that failure to be grateful is a basic human transgression. "For although they knew God, they neither glorified him as God nor gave thanks to him, but their thinking became futile and their hearts were darkened" (Romans 1:21). This text reveals a heart empty of the thankfulness that is essential in meeting God's command to be grateful.

But, does God actually command us to be grateful? The tenth commandment states "Thou shalt not covet". When you think about it, the flip side of coveting is gratitude. If I covet what someone else has it reveals I'm dissatisfied with what I have in life. On the other hand gratitude reveals I am content with God's provision and providence. The apostle Paul stated, " I have learned to be content with what ever the circumstances. I know what it is to be in need, and I know what it is to have plenty. I have learned the secret of being content in any and every situation, whether well fed or hungry, whether living in plenty or in want. I can do everything through him who gives me strength. (Philippians 4:11-13)

Paul learned to accept every situation and circumstance, even the trials and tribulations of life, as part of God's plan. Because God is sovereign, all powerful, all knowing and perfect in all his ways, he could be trusted regardless of the circumstances of life.

So thankfulness is more than just feeling good when situations and circumstances are pleasing to us; thankfulness is anchored in our faith and trust in God. If we go through trials or difficulties we know God has a purpose behind it all. James teaches us to "count it all joy" when we encounter various trials (James 1:2-4). It is through this process that God is shaping our lives and ultimately our faith may be proved genuine.

One of the themes of thanksgiving expressed over and over in the Old Testament is God's covenant faithfulness.

"Give thanks to the Lord for he is good
His love endures forever" Ps.136:1

In the New Testament we discover other reasons for offering thanks and expressing it in words of praise unto God.

"But thanks be to God who gives us the victory through our Lord Jesus Christ".
1Corinthains. 15:57

"Now thanks be to God who always leads us in triumph in Christ and through us diffuses the fragrance of his knowledge in every place". 2 Corinthians 2:14

"Giving thanks to the Father, who has qualified us to be partakers of the inheritance of the saints in light". Colossians 1:12

"For this reason we also thank God without ceasing, because when you receive the word of God which you heard from us, you welcomed it not as the word of men, but as it is in truth, the Word of God". 1 Thessalonians 2:13

"We are bound to thank God always for you, brethren, as it is fitting, because your faith grows exceedingly, and the love of every one of you all abounds towards each other".
2 Thessalonians 1:3

"But we are bound to give thanks to God always for you, beloved by the Lord, because God from the beginning choose you for salvation through sanctification by the Spirit and belief in the truth". 2 Thessalonians 2:13

"And I thank Christ Jesus our Lord who has enabled me, because he counted me faithful, putting me into the ministry". 1 Timothy 2:12

In the Christian life, we become aware that all we are and have and hope to be is a gift from God. As we celebrate our days we are filled with gratitude and express this with thanksgiving to God. Thomas Merton stated: "gratitude takes nothing for granted, is never unresponsive, is constantly awakening to new wonder, and to praise of the goodness of God." [1]

Expressing our gratitude and thanksgiving to God is a multifaceted experience. Jeff Doles [2] suggest that there are many benefits to giving thanks. Some of these are:

a. It magnifies the Lord.

"I will praise the name of the Lord with a song, and will magnify him with thanksgiving," (Psalm 69:30). When your problems appear too big for you, start declaring the praises of God, singing and giving thanks to him for who he is, and you will begin to see that God is much bigger than your problems.

b. It leads us into the presence of the Lord.

"Let us come before his presence with thanksgiving; let us sing joyfully to him with psalms" (Psalm 95:2). When you don't know where you are in your life, begin thanking and praising God and you will soon find yourself within his courts.

c. It prepares the way for blessing.

One day Jesus had a crowd of 5000 people to feed, but the resources were meagre – five loaves and two fish. However he approached this problem in faith. John tells us " Jesus took the loaves, gave thanks, and distributed to those who were seated as much as they wanted. He did the same with the fish. When they had all had enough to eat he said to his disciples, ' Gather the pieces that are left over. Let nothing be wasted.' So they gathered them and filled 12 baskets with the pieces about the five barley loaves left over by those who had eaten. (John 6:11-13).

Expressing his faith through thanksgiving, Jesus was able to feed everyone there – not only was there enough to go around, but there were 12 baskets of leftovers.

d. It paves the way for answered prayer.

Consider the raising of Lazarus from the dead. Lazarus was sick when his sisters sent word to Jesus but he was dead by the time Jesus arrived. Jesus, moved by the situation, lifted his eyes to heaven and prayed "Father, I thank you that you have heard me" (John 14:41). Even before the answer to his prayer was made evident, Jesus was giving thanks to the Father. Jesus believed he received the answer when he prayed, and so he gave thanks for it when he prayed. When he gave the word of command, "Lazarus, come forth!", the answer was made known to everyone.

e. It prepares the way for the peace of God.

There are many things in life that can cause us to feel anxious. The apostle Paul wrote " Be anxious for nothing, but in everything by prayer and supplication, with thanksgiving, let your requests be made known to God; and the peace of God which surpasses all understanding, will guard your hearts and minds through Christ Jesus" (Philippians 4:6-7). A life filled with thanksgiving is a life filled with the peace of God.

Recognising God is so intimately involved in our lives, and that he is concerned about every aspect, thanksgiving can become a way of life.

"As you therefore have received Christ Jesus the Lord, so walk in Him, rooted and built up in Him and established in the faith, as you have been taught, abounding in it with thanksgiving". (Colossians 2: 6-7)

"Whatever you do in word or deed, do all in the name of the Lord Jesus, giving thanks to God the father through Him". (Colossians 3:17)

"Rejoice always, pray without ceasing, in everything give thanks; for this is the will of God in Christ Jesus for you". (1Thessalonians 5:16-17)

"Therefore by Him let us continually offer the sacrifice of praise to God, that is, the fruit of our lips giving thanks to His name". (Hebrews 13:15)

Thomas Merton stated: "Gratitude, is more than a mental exercise, more than a formula of words. We cannot be satisfied to simply make a mental note of the things which God has done for us and then perfunctorily thanking him for favours received.

To be grateful is to recognize the love of God in everything He has given us - and He has given us everything. Every breath we draw is a gift of His love; every moment of existence is a grace. Gratitude takes nothing for granted, is never unresponsive, and is constantly awakened to new wonder and to praise of the goodness of God. For the grateful person knows that God is good, not by hearsay but by experience. That is what makes all the difference....

Gratitude is therefore the heart of a solitary life, as it is the heart of the Christian life....

We live in constant dependence upon this merciful kindness of the Father, and thus our whole life is a life of gratitude – a constant response to His help which comes to us at every moment". [3]

EXERCISE:

The exercises for this week will be based upon the theme of offering praise and thanksgiving to God for who he is and what he has done. You will have an opportunity to reflect upon various scripture passages and explore themes in the text that are similar in your life. Remember giving thanks is the 'will of God' for us. Paul wrote, "In everything give thanks; for this is the will of God in Christ Jesus for you" (1 Thessalonians 5:18)

In these exercises there will be an opportunity to reflect on seven different names of God used in the Old Testament. God has many facets to His character and each is represented by a name. These names will help you understand who God is and what He has done. Then you will be invited to explore how this name of God has been experienced in your life and with this awareness you are invited to express gratitude and thanksgiving to God.

The seven names of God to be considered are:

a. Jehovah – Jireh: (je-ho'-vah yeer'-eh) "The Lord will Provide"

b. Jehovah – Rapha: (je-ho'-vah ro'phay) "The Lord who Heals"

c. Jehovah – Nissi: (je-ho'-vah nis-see) " The Lord our Banner"

d. Jehovah – M'Kaddesh: (je-ho'-vah m'-kad'desh) "The Lord who Sanctifies"

e. Jehovah – Shalom: (je-ho'-vah shal-lom) "The Lord my Peace"

f. Jehovah – Tsidkenu: (je-ho'-vah tsid-kay'-noo) "The Lord Our Righteousness"

g. Jehovah - Rohi: (je-ho'-vah ro'ee) "The Lord Our Shepherd

DAY 1. JEHOVAH – JIREH:

DAY 1

The setting from which this name arises is Genesis 22. Here we find Abraham facing one of the greatest challenges in his life. God had promised him a child and in his old age he and Sarah his wife were able to experience the fulfillment of this promise. Now God was asking Abraham to offer his son, this child of promise as a sacrifice. God said to him, "Take your son, your only son Isaac who you love and go to the region of Moriah. Sacrifice him there as a burnt offering on one of the mountains I will tell you about." Genesis 22:2.

In obedience to God Abraham, not aware this was a test from God, takes his son Isaac, two of his young men, wood for the offering and went to the place which God told him.

After several days of travelling they saw in the distance the place God had spoken about. Abraham told the two young men to wait for him to return and with Isaac he set off, Isaac carrying the wood and he carrying the fire and the knife. As they walked along Isaac asked his father 'where is the lamb for the burnt offering?" Abraham replied " God himself will provide the lamb for the burnt offering."

As Isaac was about to be sacrificed an angel of the Lord cried out, "Abraham, Abraham! ...Do not lay a hand on the boy. ...Now I know you fear God, because you have not withheld from me your son your only son.' Abraham looked up and there in the thicket he saw a ram caught by its horns. He went over and took the ram and sacrificed it as a sacrifice as a burnt offering instead of his son. So Abraham called that place The Lord Will Provide." (Genesis 22:11-14)

'Jehovah Jireh' is a reminder of the grace of God who brought about this deliverance, but Abraham can hardly have emerged from this experience without feeling something far deeper than the testing of his faith had occurred. In fact the angel spoke a second time and told him that because of his obedience, he would be blessed, his descendents would be numerous, and through his offspring the nations of the earth would be blessed. Did he see through the eyes of faith something more?

Abraham understood the reality of sin and the need for atonement. But all sacrifices for sin were but temporary offerings for the blood of bulls and goats cannot take away sin. On this mountain God was teaching Abraham what He himself was prepared to provide. He was teaching the great cost to himself in the provision of the sacrifice for sin. Just as it would break Abraham's heart to offer up his son, his only son, consider what it cost God to offer up His son His only son as the sacrifice for the sins of the world. John wrote "God so loved the world that He gave His only son…" (John 3:16). And Paul speaks of God as "He spared not his own son but delivered him up for us all" (Romans 4:25).

Isaac would ask, "Where is the lamb?" Abraham answers "God will provide himself a lamb." John the Baptist seeing Jesus declares "Behold the Lamb of God that takes away the sin of the world" (John 1:29) It is this Lamb that is the centre of the praise and worship of heaven as the angels and elders around the throne of God sing with a loud voice,

 "Worthy is the Lamb, who was slain, to receive power and wealth and wisdom and strength and honour and glory and praise!" Then I heard every creature in heaven and on earth and on the sea, and all that is in them, singing: "To him who sits on the throne and to the lamb be praise and honour and glory and power, forever and ever!" (Revelation 5:12-13)

EXERCISE:

1. Read the story of Abraham and Isaac Genesis 22

2. What does the name 'Jehovah Jireh mean for you? How has God provided for you?

3. Apart from your 'salvation' in what other ways does God provide for you? Read Philippians 4:19. Write out your reflections.

4. Express your gratitude to God as you recall his 'provision' in your life.

DAY 2

DAY 2. JEHOVAH – RAPHA

This name means Jehovah heals. The nation of Israel had crossed the Red Sea in their bid for freedom from Egypt and now they were in the desert of Shur. After three days of being in the wilderness they found no water and began to complain. They forgot God delivered them from four hundred years of slavery and most recently from certain death as they faced the Red Sea on one side and the powerful Egyptian army on the other side. We are told they started to murmur against Moses and "when they came to Marah they could not drink its water because the water was bitter. (That is why the place was called Marah)." (Exodus 15: 23)

God showed Moses a piece of wood which he threw into the water and it turned the bitterness into sweetness and the people drank the water. They were refreshed for the journey and their murmuring was turned into praise. Then God said something rather remarkable. "If you listen to the voice of the Lord your God, and do what is right in his eyes, if you pay attention to all his commandments and keep all his decrees, I will not bring on you any of the diseases I brought upon the Egyptians, for I am the Lord who heals you." (Exodus 15:26)

God pledged on condition of their obedience to always be their 'Healer'.

In the Old and New Testament we see God's healing grace in the lives of people. Hezekiah, who was very ill, was healed and God granted him an additional number of years to live. Moses cried out to God for the healing of his sister Miriam who had leprosy. Jesus began his ministry in the synagogue where he spoke the words of the prophet Isaiah:

"The Spirit of the Lord is upon me because he has anointed me to preach good news to the poor. He has sent me to proclaim freedom for the prisoners and the recovery of sight to the blind, to release the oppressed, to proclaim the year of the Lord's favour." (Luke 4:18-19)

Wherever Jesus went the sick were brought to him. Matthew tells us, " Jesus went throughout Galilee, teaching in their synagogues, preaching the good news of the kingdom, and healing every disease and sickness among the people. News about him spread all over Syria so people brought to him all who were ill with various diseases, those suffering severe pain, the demon possessed, those having seizures, the paralyzed and he healed them. (Matthew 4:23-24)

However it is important to understand God's healing is not limited to physical problems. Jesus came to heal to every aspect of our life, which includes the brokenness of our relationship with God. Sometimes he would say to people "your sins are forgiven". To some of his critics, who challenged his association with tax collectors and sinners he declared "It is not the healthy who need a doctor but the sick. But go and learn what this means: ' I desire mercy not sacrifice.' For I have not come to call the righteous but sinners." (Matthew 9:12-13)

Just as the waters at Mara were healed by the wood being placed in it, Jesus brings healing by being placed on the wooden cross. Peter wrote: "He himself bore our sins in his body on the tree, so that we might die to sin and live for righteousness; by his wounds you have been healed." (1 Peter 2:24)

EXERCISE:

1. Read the story of the healing of the waters. Exodus 15

2. Reflect upon God's healing work in your life. Write in your journal any specific event you can remember. How has your life been changed through this experience.

3. Where do you need to experience healing now? Examine your relationship with God, with yourself, with others.

4. How will this be reflected in your prayers of thanksgiving and gratitude?

DAY 3. JEHOVAH – NISSI

DAY

3

The children of Israel would discover another aspect of God's nature; he is Jehovah – Nissi 'Jehovah my banner'.

God revealed himself as their provider and healer, now as the Israelites faced another challenge God would show himself to be their banner. In Exodus 17 the Israelites encountered their enemy the Amalekites. Although these people were direct descendents of Esau they became a persistent enemy of Israel.

Moses told Joshua to choose men and go and fight Amalek. These enemies were well equipped, well trained and outnumbered the fighting men of Israel who were ill equipped and poorly disciplined. In order to encourage Joshua and the army, Moses took a position on a hill over looking the battle field. In his hand he held the staff of God and as long as he held his hands up Israel was winning, but if his hands were lowered the Amalekites were winning. With help to support his arms, Israel eventually won the battle.

At the end of the day Moses built an altar and called it "The Lord is my Banner. For my hands were lifted up to the throne of the Lord." (Exodus 17: 15-16)

When Moses was standing on the hill with upraised hands, we see this as an act of interceding with God seeking victory over their enemy. But there is more. In his hand was the staff of God also known as the banner. A banner in biblical times was a pole with a bright ornament which would shine in the sun. As a standard, when it was raised it became a call to the people to rally around God's cause or battle. It was a sign of deliverance and of salvation.

Israel's experience with Amalek is similar to our experience in spiritual warfare. Amalek was the first enemy to appear, but they would not be the last. Symbolically, Amalek stands for the 'kingdom of this world' which is in opposition to the 'kingdom of our God'. Today Christians need to recognize they are in a spiritual battle. The enemy is aggressive and fearless. Paul writing to the church in Ephesus states very clearly,

" Put on the full armour of God so that you can take your stand against the devil's schemes. For our struggle is not against flesh and blood, but against the rulers, against the authorities, against the powers of this dark world and against the supernatural forces of evil in the heavenly realms. Therefore put on the full armour of God, so that when the day of evil comes, you may be able to stand your ground, and after you have done everything, stand. Stand firm then, with the belt of truth buckled around your waist, with the breastplate of righteousness in place, and with your feet fitted with the readiness that comes from the gospel of peace. In addition to this, take up the shield of faith, with which you can extinguish all the flaming arrows of the evil one. Take the helmet of salvation and the sword of the Spirit, which is the word of God. And pray in the Spirit on all occasions with all kinds of prayer and requests." (Ephesians 6:10-18)

We cannot fight spiritual battles on our own. When Moses became tired and his arms were lowered the Staff of God was not seen and the enemy gained ground. He needed help to keep his arms raised in order for the Staff of God to be seen and to be victorious. God's presence is absolutely essential for victory.

The staff in Moses' hand was a symbol of the mighty power of God. The cross of Christ is our banner of God's redemptive power over the forces of evil. Paul expressed it in these words. "If God is for us who can be against us. He who did not spare his own Son but gave him up for us all — how will he not also , along with him, graciously give us all things? Who shall separate us from the love of Christ? In all things we are more than conquerors though him who loved us." (Romans 8: 31-32,37)

EXERCISE:

1. Read the account of the battle in Exodus 17.

2. Read Ephesians 6: 10-18. Re-read this passage slowly and visualize putting on the various pieces of armour. This can be a daily exercise as you prepare for each day

3. Read/sing the Luther's famous hymn 'A Mighty Fortress is our God' Note the battles we face. Or read/sing the hymn 'Lift High the Cross'...

A MIGHTY FORTRESS

A mighty fortress is our God
A refuge never ending
Our helper sure amidst the flood of mortal ills prevailing.
For still our ancient foe yet seeks to work us woe
With craft and power great and,
Armed with cruel hate, on earth has not an equal.

Did we in our own strength confide,
Our striving would be losing,
Were not a Saviour on our side, the One of God's own choosing.
Who is this Saviour who? Christ Jesus, living true.
Lord Sabbaoth by name, from age to age the same,
Already wins the battle.
And though this world with evil filled,
Should threaten to undo us,
We will not fear for God has willed the truth to triumph through us:
The powers of death and hell our God will surely quell:
Their rage we can endure, for look! their doom is sure:
One little wor
d will fell them.

That Word above all earthly powers
No thanks to them! Abiding
Ensures that all God's gifts are ours, through Christ in us residing
Whose summons rings above all goods, all earthly love.
Earth's powers waste away; God's word endures always,
Whose reign will last forever.

(Martin Luther) (public domain)

LIFT HIGH THE CROSS

Lift high the cross
The love of Christ proclaim
Till all the world adore
His sacred name. (refrain)

Come Christians follow where the master trod,
Our king victorious, Christ the Son of God.

Led on their way by this triumphant sign
The hosts of God in conquering ranks combine.

Each new born servant of the Crucified
Bears on the brow the seal of Him who died.

O Lord, once lifted on the glorious tree,
Your life has brought us life eternally.

So shall our song of triumph ever be:
Praise to the Crucified for victory!
(George Kitchen)
(public domain)

4. As you prepare for the day remind yourself that the Lord is 'Jehovah – Nissi'

DAY 4. JEHOVAH - M'KADDESH

The next revelation of God's name is Jehovah - M'Kaddesh which means Jehovah who sanctifies.

This name was first revealed in Leviticus 20:7-8 when the Lord spoke to the nation of Israel. "Consecrate yourselves and be holy, because I am the Lord your God. Keep my decrees and follow them, I am the Lord, who makes you holy."

The term sanctify means to dedicate, to consecrate, to keep holy or to set apart. For example we read in Genesis the seventh day was unique because God set it apart. "By the seventh day God finished the work he had been doing, so on the seventh day God rested from all his work. And God blessed the seventh day and made it holy, because on it He rested from all the work of creating he had done." (Genesis 2:2-3)

DAY
4

In addition we discover people were also 'set apart'. Jeremiah was set apart by God to be a prophet to the nation and this was done even before Jeremiah was born. "Before I formed you in the womb I knew you. Before you were born I set you apart; I appointed you to be a prophet to the nations." (Jeremiah 1:5)

As the 'Holy One' Jehovah is set apart from all creation. And because he is holy we cannot approach him in our sinfulness. The prophet Isaiah was going to the temple to mourn the death of King Uzziah when he saw the Lord. There the seraphim cried out "Holy, holy, holy is the Lord Almighty; the whole earth is full of his glory." (Isaiah 6: 3) When Isaiah saw this he fell down and cried out, "Woe to me! I am ruined! For I am a man of unclean lips and I live among a people of unclean lips and my eyes have seen the King, the Lord Almighty". (Isaiah 6:5). From this point on Isaiah realized that the only way humankind could approach a holy God was if they were purified of all their sin.

A holy God demands holiness in his people. First and foremost this means we serve no other gods but Jehovah himself, for people become like the gods they serve. As we have repented of our sin and received Christ into our heart by faith we realize in the words of Peter that God's "divine power has given us everything we need for life and godliness through our knowledge of him who called us by his own glory and goodness. Through these he has given us the very great and precious promises, so that through them you might participate in the divine nature and escape he corruption in the world caused by evil desires." (2 Peter.1:3-4)

Since God is holy, and calls us to be holy, this means we actually participate in his nature, his character and his works. Since we have a free we will constantly choose the manner in which we live. Holiness is to be our way of life. Over and over we are exhorted in scripture to live a holy life, a life that is separated unto God.

"Therefore I urge you brothers, in view of God's mercy, to offer your bodies as living sacrifices, holy and pleasing to God - this is your spiritual act of worship. Do not conform any longer to the pattern of this world, but be transformed by the renewing of your mind. Then you will be able to test and approve what God's will is - his good, pleasing and perfect will." (Romans 12:1-2)

Ultimately God's purpose in history is that one day his church will be presented "as a radiant church, without spot or stain or wrinkle or any other blemish, but holy and blameless". (Ephesians 5:26-27)

Realizing we are the children of God and that one day we shall stand before God and see him face to face, how then shall we live out our days until that day? John clears up any mystery and clearly declares, "Now we are the children of God, and what we will be has not yet been made known. But we know that when he appears we shall be like him, for we shall see him as he is. Everyone who has this hope purifies himself, just as he is pure." (1John 3:2-3)

EXERCISE:

1. Read Isaiah 6:1-8.

2. How would you describe Isaiah's experience? What do you think discovered about the nature of God? How did it change his life?

3. How does the name Jehovah – M'kaddesh apply to your life?

4. In what sense do you see living your life' apart' for God?

5. What is needed for the church to be 'holy'?

6. Today pray for the church universal that we might be a holy people.

7. Read the words of the hymn Holy, Holy, Holy. If you know it sing it and let this be a prayer focus for today.

HOLY HOLY HOLY

Holy, holy, holy, Lord God Almighty!
Early in the morning our song of praise shall be.
Holy, holy, holy,
Merciful and mighty, God in three persons,
Blessed Trinity.

Holy, holy, holy, all the saints adore you
Casting down their golden crowns, around the glassy sea.
Cherubim and seraphim falling down before you:
You were and are and ever more
Shall be.

Holy, holy, holy, though the darkness hide you,
Though the sinful human eye your glory may not see,
You alone are holy, there is none beside you
Perfect in power in love
And purity.

Holy, holy, holy, Lord God Almighty!
All your works shall praise your name in earth and sky and sea:
Holy, holy, holy, merciful and mighty,
God in three persons
Blessed Trinity.

(public domain)

DAY 5. JEHOVAH – SHALOM

This name focuses upon the fact that Jehovah is peace.

The history of Israel reveals a 'roller coaster' spirituality in that the people were sometimes faithful to God and at other times they forgot him and followed the gods of other nations. The nation of Israel seemed to forget it was set apart as a special people to serve God and follow him completely. When they wandered away from the Lord they encountered serious problems and difficult circumstances and then in anguish they would cry out to the Lord for deliverance and commit themselves anew to serving him. This process was repeated over and over.

One such instance is found in Judges 6 when Israel was experiencing extreme oppression by the Midianites. These people oppressed the Israelites, taking their crops, forcing them to hide in caves and generally making life very miserable for them. A young man named Gideon lived in this period. One day while he was threshing wheat in a cave the angel of Jehovah appeared to him and announced that God's deliverance for the nation would occur. This deliverance would come through Gideon whom God would appoint as a leader. After some hesitation and reassurance, Gideon accepted the challenge and in faith built an altar which he called 'Jehovah-shalom' in anticipation of God's victory over the enemy and the ensuing peace that would reign.

The term 'shalom' – peace means more than the absence of conflict. The term 'shalom' most often means a sense of well being and contentment, and became a common form of greeting not only in Bible days but is used today in parts of the Middle East. In Gideon's time the people did not know peace because they were far from God - the source of all peace. Only as people are reconciled to God can they ever experience the peace God gives in terms of our relationship with him as well as the ability to live in difficult times with a sense of inner peace because they know the Lord is with them.

Jesus is referred to as 'the Prince of Peace'. He not only preached peace he also promised peace. To many whom he healed and comforted, he would say 'go in peace'. The first message of Peter following the resurrection of Jesus was the preaching of "peace by Jesus Christ"

(Acts.10:36). Jesus accomplished that peace by his death which paid the debt for our sins and reconciled us to God. Paul writing to the church at Colosse:

"For God was pleased to have all his fullness dwell in him, [Jesus] and through him to reconcile to himself all things, whether things on earth or things in heaven, by making peace through the shedding of his blood on the cross. Once you were alienated from God and were enemies in your minds because of your evil behaviour ... But now he has reconciled you by Christ's physical body through death to present you holy in his sight without blemish and free from accusation.' (Colossians 1: 19-21)

As we continue the life of faith, trusting in Christ and walking with him day by day we will continue to experience more and more of his peace. Paul exhorts the Christians living in Philippi to not become anxious about what is happening to them. And they faced difficult times as followers of Jesus. He simply told them to present their needs to God and then gave them this promise "The peace of God which transcends all understanding will guard your hearts and minds in Christ Jesus." (Philippians 4:7)

When we realize we belong to God and that he is sovereign over all the affairs of life, and we commit everything we are and have and hope to be to him, we will experience 'Jehovah – Shalom'.

EXERCISE:

1. Memorize Philippians 4:7

2. Read the prayer of St. Francis.

> *Lord make us servants of your peace:*
> *Where there is hate, may we sow love:*
> *Where there is hurt may we forgive;*
> *Where there is strife may we make one.*
>
> *Where there is doubt may we sow faith;*
> *Where all is gloom may we sow hope;*
> *Where all is night, may w sow light;*
> *Where all is tears may we sow joy.*
>
> *Jesus our Lord, may we not seek*
> *To be consoled but to console;*
> *Nor look to understanding hearts*
> *But look for hearts to understand.*

May we not look for love's return,
But seek to love unselfishly
For in our giving we receive
And in forgiving are forgiven.

Dying, we live and are reborn
Through death's dark night to endless day.
Lord make us servants of your peace,
To wake at last in heaven's light.

Amen.

(St. Francis of Assisi)

3. Read Judges 6-7, the story of Gideon.

4. Describe how you have experienced the peace of God

a. Are you reconciled with God and do you have peace with him?
b. How do you experience 'peace' in your life on a daily basis?

5. Sing the hymn 'May the Mind of Christ My Saviour'

May the mind of Christ my Saviour
Live in me from day to day
Jesus' love and power controlling
All I do and say.

May the word of God well richly
In my heart from hour to hour,
So that all may see I triumph
Only through God's power.

May the peace of God my Sovereign
Rule my life in everything,
That I may be calm to comfort
Sick and sorrowing.

May the love of Jesus fill me
As the waters fill the sea;
Christ exalting, self denying,
This is victory.

May I run the race before me,
Strong and brave to face the foe,
Looking only unto Jesus
As I onward go.

(K.Wilkinson)
(public domain)

DAY 6

DAY 6. JEHOVAH – TSIDKENU

The name Jehovah – Tsidkenu means Jehovah our righteousness.

This was spoken by the prophet Jeremiah when he spoke of a 'righteous branch' and a "King who was to appear and this is his name whereby he shall be called Jehovah our Righteousness" (Jeremiah 23:5-6)

The word tsidkenu is used in the sense of rendering justice and making things right. In the Old Testament the judges were warned against perverting righteous judgment. However as we look at this term it is very difficult to convey the full meaning of the word except as we look at the character of God.

Jehovah is himself perfect righteousness, and in contrast to this we see the evil ways of humanity and the lack of righteousness. The psalmist presents God as one who is looking from heaven upon humanity to see if there are any who understand his ways and who seek to do good. His conclusion is there is none.

"The Lord looks down from heaven on the sons of men to see if there is any who understand, any who seek God. All have turned aside, they have together become corrupt; there is no one who does good, not even one." (Ps.14:2-3)

The apostle Paul, quoting this passage in the New Testament, says:

"There is no one righteous, not even one; there is no one who understands, no one who seeks God. All have turned away; they have together become worthless; there is no one who does good, not even one. ... Therefore no one will be declared righteous no not one...for all have sinned and fall short of the glory of God." (Romans 3:10-12, 20, 23)

Jesus Christ, who is the full revelation of God, is the only righteous one. He is our Jehovah – Tsidkenu. In his humanity he lived up to the perfect standard of God's law, so his righteousness met all the demands of law. As one with the Father, his righteousness was a complete manifestation of the righteousness of God.

It is through Jesus Christ we are able to become righteous. Paul writes:

"God made him who had no sin to be sin for us, so that in him we might become the righteousness of God." (2Corinthians 5:21)

Peter expands upon this and declares:

"Christ died for sins once for all, the righteous for the unrighteous, to bring you to God." (1 Peter 3:18)

It is through Christ and his atoning death that we are made acceptable to God. We are clothed with the righteousness of Jehovah –our righteousness.

EXERCISE:

1. Meditate on Romans 3:23 "for all have sinned and fallen short of the glory of God". Take some time to reflect on this verse and note how this applies to your life. How have you fallen short of God's expectations?

2. What does it mean for you to be clothed in the 'righteousness of Christ'? How did this occur?

3. How does this affect your daily living? How do you seek to live 'righteously'?

4. Read and meditate upon this psalm.

PSALM 130

Out on the depths I cry to you, O Lord;
O Lord, hear my voice.
Let your ears be attentive
To my cry for mercy.

If you, O Lord, kept a record of sins,
O Lord, who could stand?
But what if you there is forgiveness;
Therefore you are feared.

I wait for the Lord, my soul waits,
And in his a word I put my hope.
My soul waits for the Lord
More than watchmen wait for the morning
More than watchmen wait for the morning

O Israel, put your hope in the Lord,
For with the Lord is unfailing love
And with him is full redemption.
He himself will redeem Israel
From all their sins.

DAY 7

DAY 7. JEHOVAH – ROHI

The name Jehovah – Rohi means Jehovah my shepherd. This is the name of God that comes from Psalm 23 and the one psalm most have committed to memory.

This psalm has brought comfort to people throughout the ages as they have faced difficult situations and as they learn to trust in God's abiding care. Jehovah is seen as the shepherd who cares for his flock and David the one who penned this name, personally experienced the constant care of God over his life.

Repeatedly the scriptures speak of God as the shepherd of his people. Isaiah the prophet writes:

"See, the sovereign Lord comes with power,
and his arm rules for him.
See, his reward is with him,
And his recompense accompanies him.
He tends his flock like a shepherd:
He gathers the lambs in his arms
And carries them close to his heart;
He gently leads those that have young." (Isaiah 40:10-11)

Ezekiel also gives us a picture of this relationship. Expressing great indignation at false shepherds, Jehovah is presented as the true shepherd who will search for his sheep and seek them out.

"This is what the sovereign Lord says: I am against the shepherds and will hold them accountable for my flock. I will remove them from attending the flock so that the shepherds can no longer feed themselves. I will rescue my flock from their mouths, and it will no longer be food for them.

For this is what the sovereign Lord says: I myself will search for my sheep and look after them.

As a shepherd looks after his scattered flock when he is with them, so will I look after my sheep. I will rescue them from all the places where they were scattered on a day of clouds and darkness

I will bring them out from the nations and gather them from the countries, and I will bring them into their own land. I will pasture them on the mountains of Israel, in the ravines and in all the settlements in the land.

I will tend them in a good pasture, and the mountain heights that Israel will be their grazing land. There they will lie down in a good grazing land, and there they will be fed in a rich pasture on the mountains of Israel.

I myself will tend my sheep and have them lie down, declares the Lord.

I will search for the lost and bring back the strays. I will bind up the injured and strengthen the weak, but the sleek and a strong I will destroy. I will shepherd the flock with justice." (Ezekiel 34:10-16)

In the New Testament the name Jehovah – Rohi is most fully realized in the person of Jesus. He declared "I am the good shepherd" (John 10:11). Those who heard him knew he was referring to the shepherd the prophet Isaiah spoke about. Jesus had a heart of compassion and he spoke about his people as sheep without a shepherd. He told a parable about a man who had 100 sheep but one of them was lost. What would he do, count his losses and get on with life? No! The shepherd goes and searches for the one lost sheep, brings it home and celebrates. That is the way God cares for us.

But there is more. Jehovah our shepherd will meet every need that we have. For those who trust him he will guide them in the right way, he will protect them from all harm, they are safe in his presence, and when wounded he will heal them with his tender care

EXERCISE:

1. Read Psalm 23. Commit this passage to memory.

2. In your prayer this day remember those who are far away from God and believe there is no hope for them. May they come to realize the "Good Shepherd" is looking for them.

3. For those who are dying may they live these last days in the knowledge that 'even when they walk through the valley of the shadow of death' they do not need to be afraid. The Lord is with them.

4. Offer the following prayer.

Lord God, your love makes us realize that we need your love and grace.
So we bring our prayers to you:
For those who suffer pain;
For those who have not had the opportunity to realize their potentialities;
For those who are satisfied with something less than the life for which they were made;
For those who know their guilt, their shallowness, their need, but do not know of Jesus;
For those who know they must soon die;
For those who cannot wait to die.

Lord God, your Son has taken all our sufferings upon himself and has transformed them.
Help us as we offer these prayers to become agents of your transforming love.
Through Jesus Christ our Lord.
Amen. (4)

Endnotes:

1. Thomas Merton, Thoughts in Solitude (New York: The Noonday Press) 1996. pg. 24.

2. Jeff Doles, The Power of Giving Thanks (Walking Barefoot Ministries Seffner Fl) 2004. pg. 6-8.

3. Thomas Merton. op.cit. pg. 56

4. Caryl Micklem. Contemporary Prayers for Public Worship (Grand Rapids Michigan: Eerdmans Publishing Co.) 1967. pg. 56.

PRAYING THROUGH
THE CHRISTIAN YEAR

Through the ages, the people of God developed a calendar of feasts to celebrate God's saving acts in history, or as Whalen states "it seeks to hold in tensive balance, time as an incarnational and eschatological balance". [1]

In the Pentateuch there were three feasts: Passover, the Feast of Weeks also called Pentecost, and the Feast of Tabernacles. The New Testament records that Jesus and the early Christians took part in these celebrations. The other Feasts mentioned in the Old Testament are the Feast of Atonement, the Feast of Unleavened Bread, the New Year Feast, and the Feast of Purim, which were held on a yearly basis.

In the New Testament, the celebrations centre around the birth, life and death of the Lord Jesus. The major events are Advent, Christmas/Epiphany, Lent, Holy Week, Easter and Pentecost. Many of these events have been recognized and celebrated by the church since the fourth century. At the time of the Reformation the Christian year fell into disuse, however in recent years there has been a growing interest in the church to find some way of ordering the church year and celebrating these significant events. Some in the evangelical church are more resistant and sceptical of this type of celebration and perhaps rightly so, since there is the possibility of misuse. In this regard, Leonard gives a word of caution and direction.

"The New Testament records no liturgical calendar and gives no directives for observing annual feasts. The apostle Paul expresses an indifference to the observance of special days; whether a believer keeps them should be a matter of personal conviction, for the purpose of glorifying and thanking the Lord (Romans 14:5-6). Historically, however the Christian church has found special value in the annual festivals as encouragements to the believer's identification with God's action of deliverance in Jesus Christ". [2]

If we are to celebrate the church year we must keep in mind the purpose of such action.

The following is a brief description of the major Christian celebrations throughout the calendar year followed by some exercise that will help to guide your prayers and devotional practices during the year. Historically the Christian year begins with the death and resurrection of Christ, however we begin the church year with the celebration of Advent ... a time of preparation for the coming of Christ.

ADVENT:

Advent (which means coming) is a time when we celebrate the coming of Christ in a threefold manner; as the promised Messiah, as the Saviour who lives in our hearts, and finally in anticipation as the One who will come again to judge the world and ultimately rule in righteousness and truth. This season first celebrated in the sixth century, begins four weeks before Christmas. During this time the church focuses upon the themes of hope, anticipation and longing. This is very similar to the Israelites as they waited in expectation for the coming Messiah. So too we look ahead for the fulfillment of the promise that the Lord will return.

CHRISTMAS:

We have no knowledge when Christ's birth occurred. It is mentioned in the gospels of Matthew and Luke and historically the church has celebrated December 25 to mark the occasion. This date was chosen to counter the celebration of the Roman winter festival which celebrated winter solstice or the lengthening of the sun. Some Christians objected to this since they feared people would confuse the celebration of the son of God with the sun god.
This celebration is a wonderful time to focus on the reality that the "Word became flesh and lived for a while among us. We have seen his glory" (John 1:14). In Jesus Christ there is the mystery of Immanuel "God with us".

EPIPHANY:

The term Epiphany means manifestation or revelation. Originally this celebration focused on the baptism of Jesus as the 'beloved son', however by the fourth century it celebrated the revelation of Jesus to the world as represented by the 'magi', men who traveled from the east to come and worship the King. This was in fulfilment of the prophesy by Isaiah. "Nations will come to your light…and kings to the brightness of your dawn…" (Isaiah 60:1-6).

LENT:

Epiphany concludes with the season of Lent, a time of personal and corporate spiritual renewal through self examination. Some scholars believe the observance of Lent may have begun as a period of fasting for candidates in preparation for baptism at Easter. It was a period of forty days that began with the imposition of ashes, a sign of our mortality and moves through the next five weeks to the climax of Palm Sunday which marks the beginning of Holy Week. Since Sundays were not considered fast days the beginning of Lent was moved back to Ash Wednesday to accommodate the forty day period.

HOLY WEEK:

Holy Week which commemorates the life of Jesus, is actually a part of the Lenten season. During this time the church reflects upon the 'passion' of Christ, his suffering and death. In the scriptures we read of his struggle in the garden of Gethsemane asking the Father to 'remove the cup', we see his betrayal by a disciple, and we try to grasp the cruel agony of death by crucifixion.

A. PALM SUNDAY:

Holy Week begins with Jesus triumphal entry into Jerusalem where he is hailed as the 'the Son of David', 'The King of Israel', and the people cry out 'Hosanna! This cry comes from the words of the psalmist:

> "O Lord save us:
> O Lord grant us success.
> Blessed is he who comes in the name of the Lord.
> From the house of the Lord we bless you." (Psalm 118:25-26)

B. MAUNDY THURSDAY:

On that final week prior to his death Jesus gathered with his disciples in an upper room to celebrate the Passover. During this celebration Jesus took a basin of water and a towel and washed the disciple's feet, an act they were not prepared to do for one another. At the conclusion of the foot washing Jesus said to them; "I your Lord and Teacher have washed your feet, you should also wash one another's feet. I have set you an example.... A new commandment I give to you, love one another as I have loved you" John 13:14-15,34). Thus the church began this celebration 'Maundy Thursday' from the Latin (mandatum novum) which translates 'a new commandment'. This commandment to love was visibly demonstrated by Jesus in the act of foot washing and as he left that place he would go to the cross, the place of ultimate sacrifice and love.

C. GOOD FRIDAY:

Good Friday, originally called 'God's Friday' is a curious term. Webber explains it. "In terms of Jesus' own pain and suffering, it was not a good day. But in view of the death of Jesus as a day when the powers of evil were put to flight and dethroned, it was a good day. Our celebration of that day in worship captures the tension of both the sorrow we bring to the day through our identification with Jesus and the joy we experience knowing that his death was the death of death, the ruination of the powers of evil." [3]

121

Today in most Christian churches Good Friday is seen as a time to reflect upon the death of Christ and the act of atonement for our sins. It is a time of solemn reflection, mixed with certain hope.

EASTER:

Easter is the most joyous season of the Christian year. Christ is Risen! Hallelujah!
We celebrate that Christ has broken the chains of death and that by his resurrection from the dead, we too shall be raised to new life. Paul expressed it in this manner: "but Christ has indeed been raised from the dead, the first fruits of those who have fallen asleep. For since death came through a man, the resurrection from the dead comes through a man. For as in Adam all die, so in Christ will all be made alive." (1 Corinthians 15:20-22).

PENTECOST:

Pentecost (meaning fiftieth) is the term for the Feast of Weeks celebrated in the Old Testament, fifty days after Passover. In the New Testament, following his resurrection, Jesus remained on earth for forty days before his ascension and commanded his disciple to wait for the coming of the Holy Spirit. Ten days after his ascension, the Spirit descended upon the church and the people began to openly proclaim Jesus as Lord and Saviour. On that day thousands were converted and the church sprang to life, empowered by the Spirit of the risen Christ.

ORDINARY TIME:

The Christian Year which is an attempt to mark in a sequential fashion the major events in the life of Christ ends with Pentecost. The time between Pentecost and advent is referred to as the Season after Pentecost or Ordinary Time. This is not to imply that it is an insignificant period but rather the focus is on the church's mission and witness to the world.

EXERCISES

ADVENT

1. *Read the account of Mary and the annunciation of the birth of Christ. Luke 1:26-38; 46-55. How can you enter into Mary's celebration expressed in verses 46-55?*

2. *Read the account of John the Baptist (Matthew 3:1-3) and his ministry of preparing people to receive the Messiah?*

3. How do you live in expectation of the return of the Lord?

4. Sing/reflect on the hymn Come O Long Expected Jesus. How does this hymn voice your longing for the coming of Christ?

COME O LONG EXPECTED JESUS

Come O long expected Jesus, born to set your people free!
From our fears and sins release us; Christ in whom our rest shall be.

Israel's strength and consolation, born salvation to impart,
Dear desire of every nation, joy of every longing heart.

Born your people to deliver, born a child and yet a king;
Born to reign in us forever, now your gracious kingdom bring.

By your own eternal Spirit rule in all our hearts alone;
By your all sufficient merit raise us to your glorious throne!

(Charles Wesley)
public domain

CHRISTMAS

1. Read Isaiah 9:2-7 and Isaiah 52: 7-10. Take some time to meditate upon the reality that the Prince of Peace has come to us and brings the message of peace.

2. How does this message of peace bring hope to your life, community the world?

3. Reflect upon the following hymn.

O Come O Come Emmanuel

O come, O come, Emmanuel and ransom captive Israel
Who mourns in lonely exile here until the son of God draws near.
Rejoice, rejoice, Emmanuel shall come to you
O Israel!
O come true Branch of Jesse, free your children from this tyranny;
From depths of hell your people save, to raise victorious from the grave.

123

4. Offer the following Christmas prayer

Heavenly Father
We give you praise for the ordinariness of Christmas –
That the day comes the same as any other day.
We give you praise that there is no sign in the heavens, and no bright star but the light
of your presence in the ordinary birth of a child.
We give you praise that you are the centre of human affairs, involved in the struggle of
life and sharing human experience.
We give you praise that out of compassion you take our part and open to us a new way
of life. We pray that this day we shall be able to see its true glory.
Through Jesus Christ our Lord.
Amen. [4]
(adapted)

7. Conclude your time by sitting in silence for five minutes and then give thanks to God for his presence in your life.

EPIPHANY

1. Read the account of the visit of the Magi in Matthew 2: 1-12

2. Pray that the gospel of Christ will be proclaimed throughout the world. Remember Christian brothers and sisters in various parts of the world that are experiencing great difficulty and hardship for the sake of the gospel. Remember and meditate upon the words of Jesus: "Blessed are those who are persecuted because of righteousness, for theirs is the kingdom of heaven" (Matthew 5:10)

3. Reflect upon this hymn as it speaks to us about Jesus who brings light to dispel the darkness.

AS WITH GLADNESS MEN OF OLD

As with gladness men of old did the guiding star behold;
As with joy they hailed its light, leading onward beaming bright:
So most gracious Lord may we, evermore be drawn to thee.

As with joyful steps they sped, Saviour to thy lowly bed,
There to bend the knee before thee, whom heaven and earth adore,
So may we with wiling feet, ever seek thy mercy seat.

As they offered gifts most rare at thy cradle rude and bare.
So may we with holy joy, pure and free from sins alloy,
All our costliest treasures bring, Christ to thee our heavenly King.

Holy Jesus every day keep us in the narrow way,
And when earthly things are past, bring our ransomed souls at last
Where they need no star to guide, where no clouds of glory hide.

In that heavenly country bright need they no created light:
Thou its light, its joy, its crown, thou its sun which goes not down,
There forever may we sing hallelujahs to our king.

(William Dix)
public domain

4. Offer the following prayer. At the conclusion remain in silence.

Almighty God, at this season of Epiphany we are confronted again with Jesus
Christ the light of the world.
We stop amidst all the activity of this day to reflect upon your presence in our lives.
We are also aware that many people struggle and stumble around in the darkness of
life. May we not selfishly keep the light unto ourselves, but willingly reflect you to
others.
Help us to seize every opportunity that comes to us … through our actions and
words may we mirror your presence as we share the wonderful story of Christ with
everyone we meet.
Give us courage and boldness that our ministry may be used to spread the good
news of Jesus Christ to all.
This we pray in the name of Jesus Christ, the light of the world.
Amen.

LENT

1. Read Joel 2:1-2; 12-17. Reflect upon the penitential desire of the people.

2. Prayer for the beginning of Lent.

125

Lord God, as we remember the temptation, suffering and death of Jesus Christ,
help us to take up the cross and follow him.

Save us O God from the hurt and pride that leads to anger so that we nurse our
grudges and resentments and refuse to love and forgive.
By the power of the Holy Spirit help us to do as Jesus did – love our enemies, pray
for our persecutors and forgive others the wrongs they have done.

Save us O God from the self - centredness that makes us blind to the needs of others.
By the power of the Holy Spirit help us to live as Jesus lived –
Always ready to listen, never too tired to help, always living not for ourselves but
for you and others.

Lord God, save us from the selfishness that turns us in on ourselves so that we put
ourselves first and push other people out of our way.
By the power of the Holy Spirit help us to do as Jesus did –
Leave self behind, and take up the cross.

We pray this in the name of God the Father, Son and Holy Spirit.
Amen.[5]
(adapted)

*3. Attend a church service where you can participate in the Ash Wednesday service.
What does it mean to you to hear these words "From the earth you came, to the
earth you shall return" as the ashes are imposed on your forehead?*

*4. Take some time to reflect on your life. Ask the Lord to reveal areas of your life that
He desires to change. Confess to God those sins that you are aware of. Celebrate
the mercy and grace of God.*

PALM SUNDAY

1. Read the account of Jesus' triumphal entry into Jerusalem. (Matthew 21:1-11)

2. Reflect upon the hymn.

HOSANNA LOUD HOSANNA

Hosanna, loud hosanna, the little children sang; through pillared court and temple the joyful anthem rang.
To Jesus, who had held them close folded to his breast, the children sang their praises the simplest and the best.

From Olivet they followed amid the shouting crowd, the victor palm branch waving and chanting clear and loud.
Messiah, God's anointed, rode there in humble state, "Hosanna in the highest!". Rang out their praises great.

"Hosanna in the highest!" that ancient song we sing for Christ is our Redeemer. The Lord of heaven our King.
Oh may we ever praise him with heart and life and voice, and in God's joyful presence eternally rejoice.

(Jennette Threlfall)
public domain

3. Reflect and meditate upon this prayer.

Lord Jesus, when you entered Jerusalem, people shouted "Blessed are you who comes in the name of the Lord. Hosanna in the highest".
Lord we want to join them in their welcome and praise.

When the people's praise turned into jeering and they shouted "Crucify him", you prayed for their forgiveness.
Lord Jesus, we are the same sort of people as those who jeered and we need your forgiveness as well.

When you were raised from the dead, people were brought to see in your living and dying the surpassing love of God.
We are grateful O Lord that nothing can separate us from the love of God which we find in you.

Praise and honour, glory and might, be to Him who sits on the throne and to the lamb, forever and ever.
Amen [6]
(adapted)

MAUNDY THURSDAY

1. Read the account of Jesus act of servanthood as he washed the disciple's feet. John 13:1-17.

2. Read and meditate upon the hymn.

A NEW COMMANDMENT

A new commandment I give unto you, that you love one another as I have loved
you, that you love one another as I have loved you.
By this shall all know you are my disciples: if you have love one for another;
By this shall all know you are my disciples if you have love; one for another.

(public domain)

3. Offer the following prayer.

Lord Jesus,
Although you were the master, you washed the feet of the disciples
and acted as the servant.
Make us servants to one another. Take away all pride and vain ambition and give us
a spirit of humility so that we may serve not only you but also one another. Give us
Lord Jesus your attitude:
"Who being in very nature God, did not could equality with God something to be
grasped, but made himself nothing, taking the very nature of a servant, being made
in human likeness.
And being found in appearance as a man, he humbled himself and became obedient
to death - even death on a cross!
Therefore God exalted him to the highest place and gave him the name that is
above every name, that at the name of Jesus every knee should bow, in heaven and
earth and under the earth, and every tongue confess that Jesus Christ is lord, to the
glory of God the Father". (Philippians 2:6-11)

Amen.

GOOD FRIDAY

1. Read the prophetic words of Isaiah. 53:1-12. Read the account of the crucifixion of Jesus Mark 15:1-41.

2. Meditate upon the prayer for Good Friday

PRAYER FOR GOOD FRIDAY

O God, we were not there when they crucified Jesus. But we are here today and we can imagine and visualize in our own way the the pain and suffering of our Lord.
We have attempted to view history and dismiss any personal involvement or guilt by boldly asserting we would never have acted that way.
Yet, we did and still do!
As much as we try, we are not able to escape the truth that we have contributed to Christ's death on the cross.
It is for our sins and stubborn rebellion that he died on this day.
God, forgive our weak and vacillating faith, which is more conditioned and controlled by the pressure of the crowds than the presence of Christ.
Replay the crucifixion in our minds so that we might see your wounded out-stretched hands of love.
Lift the shadows of sin and allow us to experience the redeeming goodness and mercy of Good Friday.
Through Jesus Christ, the great shepherd of our souls.
Amen. [7](adapted)

3. Sing the hymn Beneath the Cross of Jesus

BENEATH THE CROSS OF JESUS

Beneath the cross of Jesus, I fain would take my stand, the shadow of a might rock within a weary land, a home within the wilderness, a rest upon the way , from the burning of the noontide heat and the burden of the day.

Upon the cross of Jesus mine eyes at times can see the very dying form of one who suffered there for me, and from my stricken heart with tears two wonders I confess: the wonder of redeeming love and my own unworthiness.
I take O cross thy shadow for my abiding place; I ask no other sunshine than the sunshine of thy face, content to let the world go by, to know no gain or loss; my sinful self my only shame, my glory all the cross.
(Elizabeth Celphane)
public domain

129

EASTER

THE LORD IS RISEN!
HE IS RISEN INDEED!
ALLELUIA!

1. Sing the Easter hymn Jesus Christ is Risen Today

JESUS CHRIST IS RISEN TODAY

Jesus Christ is risen today hallelujah, our triumphant holy day hallelujah!
Who did once upon the cross hallelujah, suffer to redeem our loss hallelujah!

Hymns of praise then let us sing, hallelujah, unto Christ our heavenly king, hallelujah!
Who endured the cross and grave, hallelujah sinners to redeem and save, hallelujah!

But the pains which he endured, hallelujah, our salvation have procured hallelujah!
Now above the sky he's king, hallelujah, where the angels ever sing, hallelujah!

Sing we to our God above, hallelujah, praise eternal as his love, hallelujah!
Praise him all ye heavenly host, hallelujah, Father, Son and Holy Ghost, hallelujah!
Amen.
(Charles Wesley)
public domain

2. Read Matthew's account of the resurrection. (Matthew 28:1-5)

3. Declare your belief in the words of the creed.

APOSTLE'S CREED

I believe in God the Father almighty,
Creator of heaven and earth.
I believe in Jesus Christ, God's only Son our Lord,
Who was conceived by the Holy Spirit,
Born of the Virgin Mary,
Suffered under Pontius Pilate,

Was crucified, died and was buried;

He descended to the dead.

On the third day he rose again;

He ascended into heaven,

He is seated at the right hand of the Father,

And he will come to judge the living and the dead.

I believe in the Holy Spirit,

The holy catholic Church,

The communion of saints,

The forgiveness of sins,

The resurrection of the body,

And the life everlasting.

Amen

PENTECOST

1. Read Acts. 2: 1-21 that speaks of the birth of the church or Ezekiel 37:1-14 where the prophet address the new life given by the Spirit of God.

2. Pray for God's empowering of your life.

Spirit of God, powerful and unpredictable as the wind,

As you came upon the followers of Jesus on that first

Pentecost and swept them off their feet,

So that they found themselves doing what they never

dreamed to be possible in their lives.

It is you, Spirit of God, who through the ages have enabled men and women to go about this world telling of the good news of Jesus and serving people even as he did.

Spirit of God, powerful and unpredictable as the wind,

Come upon us and empower us for living every day.

Amen. [8]

(adapted)

public domain

3. Sing/read the hymn Spirit of God

SPIRIT OF GOD

Spirit of God descend upon my heart wean it from earth through all its pulses move.
Stoop to my weakness mighty as thou art, and make me love you as I ought to love.

I ask no dream no prophet ecstasies, no sudden rending of the veil of clay.
No angel messenger, no opening skies, but take the dimness of my soul away.

Hast thou not bid me love thee God and King? All thine own soul, heart and
strength and mind;
I see thy cross there teach my heart to cling: oh let me seek thee and oh let me find.

Teach me to feel that thou art always nigh; teach me the struggles of the soul to bear
To face the rising doubt the rebels sigh; teach me the patience of unanswered prayer.

Teach me to love thee as thine angels love, one holy passion filling all my frame:
The baptism of the heaven descended Dove, my heart an altar and thy love the flame.

Amen
(George Croly)
public domain

ORDINARY TIME

1. Read John 17. Make this text the basis for your prayer as you seek to extend the work of Christ in the world.

2. Conclude with the praying of the Lord Prayer.

Our Father in Heaven
Hallowed be your name
You kingdom come
Your will be done
On earth as it is in heaven.
Give us today our daily bread
Forgive us our debts
As we also have forgiven our debtors
And lead us not into temptation
But deliver us from evil
Amen
(Matthew 6:9-13)

3. Sing/read the hymn, I the Lord of Sea and Sky.

I THE LORD OF SEA AND SKY

I the Lord of sea and sky, I have heard my people cry,
All who dwell in dark and sin, my hand will save.
I who made the stars of night, I will make their darkness bright.
Who will bear my light to them? Whom will I Send?
(refrain)

Here I am Lord. Is it I Lord?
I have heard you calling in the night.
I will go Lord if you lead me.
I will hold your people in my heart.

I the Lord of snow and rain, I have borne my people's pain.
I have wept for love of them: they turn away.
I will break their hearts of stone, give them hearts for love alone.
I will speak my word to them. Whom shall I send?

I the Lord of wind and flame, I will tend the poor and lame.
I will set a feast for them: my hand will save.
Finest bread I will provide till their hearts be satisfied.
I will give my life to them. Whom will I send?

(Daniel Schutte)
public domain

WEEK EIGHT

_____

_____

_____

_____

_____

_____

_____

_____

_____

_____

_____

_____

_____

_____

_____

_____

_____

_____

_____

_____

_____

_____

_____

Endnotes:

1. Michael Whalen, Seasons and Feasts of the Church Year (New York: Paulist Press) 1993 pg. 7

2. Robert Webber (editor), The Complete Library of Worship Volume 1 (Nashville: Star Song Publishing Group) 1993 pg. 194

3. Robert Webber, Ancient Future Time (Grand Rapids: Baker) 2004 pg. 130

4. Carl Micklem, Contemporary Prayers for Public Worship (Grand Rapids:Eerdmans) 1967 pg 113

5. ibid. pg. 115

6. ibid. pg. 118

7. Robert Webber (editor) The Complete Library of Worship op.cit. pg 290.

8. Carl Micklem op.cit. pg. 131

CPSIA information can be obtained at www.ICGtesting.com
Printed in the USA
BVOW07s0555290415

397902BV00029B/225/P